Understanding Schematic
Learning at Two

Also available from Bloomsbury

Early Childhood Studies, Ewan Ingleby
Good Practice in the Early Years, edited by Janet Kay
Personal, Social and Emotional Development, Pat Broadhead, Jane Johnston,
Caroline Tobbell and Richard Woolley
Physical Development, Linda Cooper
Understanding Schemas in Young Children, Stella Louis, Clare Beswick,
Liz Magraw and Lisa Hayes, edited by Sally Featherstone

Understanding Schematic Learning at Two

Julie Brierley and Cathy Nutbrown

Bloomsbury Academic
An imprint of Bloomsbury Publishing Plc

B L O O M S B U R Y
LONDON · OXFORD · NEW YORK · NEW DELHI · SYDNEY

Bloomsbury Academic

An imprint of Bloomsbury Publishing Plc

50 Bedford Square	1385 Broadway
London	New York
WC1B 3DP	NY 10018
UK	USA

www.bloomsbury.com

BLOOMSBURY and the Diana logo are trademarks of Bloomsbury Publishing Plc

First published 2017

British Library Cataloguing-in-Publication Data

A catalogue record for this book is available from the British Library.

ISBN:	HB:	978-1-4742-5754-1
	ePDF:	978-1-4742-5755-8
	ePub:	978-1-4742-5756-5

Library of Congress Cataloging-in-Publication Data

A catalog record for this book is available from the Library of Congress.

Typeset by Integra Software Services Pvt. Ltd.
Printed and bound in Great Britain

To Joe, Hannah & Scott – all my love (JB)
For Ruby – who is delightfully curious about the world (CEN)

Contents

List of Figures

About the Authors

Dr Julie Brierley is a lecturer at the University of Hull. She teaches on a range of early childhood courses. Julie originally qualified and worked as Primary School teacher working mainly in Trafford Education Authority. After the birth of her own children, she moved to North Yorkshire and along with her husband took over the ownership and management of a private day nursery. It is from this her interest in younger children, especially two-year-old children developed. Julie's interest in children's active movement and schema continued to grow as she studied for her MA and EdD at The University of Sheffield. Julie continues to work with practitioners and parents through her children's day nursery. This is Julie's first book and she'd like to thank Cathy Nutbrown for having the confidence to believe in her, and for all her support as a co-author of this book.

Professor Cathy Nutbrown is Director of the Early Childhood Education at The University of Sheffield where she teaches on a range of early years undergraduate, masters and doctoral programmes. She is author of over fifty publications in the field of early Childhood Education, including *Threads of Thinking: Schemas and Young Children*. In 2011/2012 she chaired the Nutbrown Review, an independent review of Early Education and Childcare Qualifications, *Foundations for Quality*. In 2013 she won an ESRC prize Outstanding Impact in Society for her research and in the same year was awarded a Nursery World Lifetime Achievement Award.

Acknowledgements

To learn more about young children requires us to spend time with them, to become involved in their life and share their experiences.

Julie expresses her sincere thanks to the parents and children who selflessly allowed her into their lives; it is through their generosity that this book exists. We both want to recognize the practitioners who skilfully support young children and their exploits on a daily basis.

Introduction

High-quality early childhood education can make all the difference to children's well-being and success in school and later life. Yet there still remains a general lack of research into two-year-olds and their learning in comparison to studies focusing on children aged three and over. This book focuses specifically on two-year-olds learning using rich case study material to understand their schematic learning and to consider how focusing deeply on what these amazing learners do might provide a key to understanding their learning.

Various authors have offered a range of definitions of schemas and we explore their interpretations throughout the book. We want to resist, from the outset, offering simplistic and shorthand definitions of schemas, so for readers new to schemas we point now to Athey's work which began modern interest in young children's schematic learning. We shall come to this again later in the book when we consider some examples of young children's schematic behaviour; Athey (2007: 5) describes a schema as a 'pattern of repeatable actions that lead behaviour and thinking in children that exists underneath the surface features of various contents, contexts and specific experiences'. What is important here is that observable, repeatable patterns of behaviour are noted by practitioners and parents who can then offer children content, contexts and experiences which match and nourish those patterns (or schemas) in order to support learning. Following on from Athey's definition, Nutbrown (2011) suggests that it is from these early patterns of behaviour that the foundations of young children's learning can be observed and supported, and that is what this book is about.

Atherton and Nutbrown (2013) highlighted the significance and importance of recognizing schema as a tool for interpreting young children's thinking and understanding of the world, and how schematic pedagogy might support practitioners to work, in tune with the youngest children (Atherton and

Nutbrown 2016). This book covers relatively unexplored territory focusing specifically on the needs and interests of two-year-olds and their learning, in a nursery setting and in their homes. It offers practical insights for working with toddlers and shows how young children's involvement with materials and the environment supports their schematic development.

Drawing on research to highlight the important links between learning opportunities, environment and the role of the adults, the book foregrounds how young children learn. It demonstrates how understanding and valuing young children's schemas provides adults with opportunities to acknowledge two-year-old children's capability to actively construct and develop an understanding of the world they live in.

This book aims to offer a deeper insight into how two-year-old children learn and how a schematic pedagogy can be used first to recognize and then to develop two-year-old children's thinking and understanding of the world around them. Focusing, in Part Two, on four children over a sixteen-week period, their individual experiences and stories at home and in a nursery setting are constructed. Julie observed Abby, Hannah, Emily and George in their nursery setting and their homes and the detail of those observations offers a greater understanding of how even at such a young age children are intrinsically motivated to select resources from the environment to support their schematic thinking. Detailed observational and photographic evidence unfolds the children's schematic learning journeys. The book foregrounds the appropriate environment and pedagogy required to support two-year-old children's schematic explorations and development.

Part One

The Early Years: Research, Policy and Theory

Young children's questioning minds are pivotal to their learning. When they explore and experiment in environments that stimulate their thinking and questioning, they drive their own learning in ways that adult-directed learning hardly ever could. Whilst much has been written about the learning and thinking of three- to five-year-olds, the same cannot be said for children under three, and the mysteries and magic of the learning of two-year-olds is still largely to be discovered.

Since the works of Piaget (1953) and Isaacs (1930) in the first part of the twentieth century, we have understood something more of young children's self-generated questions (particularly of three- to six-year-olds); and we now know of the importance of creating supportive environments – filled with materials to explore and adults to help children in their self-chosen explorations. It was Nathan Isaacs who took an interest in children's 'why' questions (Isaacs 1930: 291–349) and he believed that children needed opportunities to explore their own answers to those questions with the support of adults (Graham 2009). Susan Isaacs (1930: 158) based much of her pedagogical approach on cycles of life, birth and death. She wrote that 'an active, continuous and cumulative interest in animal and plant life – but particularly animal – develops easily and uninterruptedly out of the little child's impulses of curiosity and pleasure in these things, given certain conditions' she promoted the practice of following the child's interest and providing materials and an environment which enabled them to find answers to their questions.

Of course, when children have more developed language they can articulate the kinds of questions that Isaacs's children in the Malting House might have asked – such as 'Is the Rabbit dead?' 'If we put it in water it might come back to life?' In this book, the two-year-olds that Julie has observed are still at the point where they understand many, many more words that they say. They seem to be forming questions, but they are not yet able to express them verbally. Julie, and the other practitioners in the nursery adopt a pedagogy of listening (Scott 1996) whereby they attune to each child and try to listen to their learning and thinking in ways that do not depend wholly on the spoken word. In practice akin to the *Hundred Languages of Childhood* adopted in the Reggio Emilia preschools and infant toddler centres (Edwards et al. 2011), Julie, the practitioners and the parents of Abby, Hannah, Emily and George (the children who will feature in Part Two of the book) 'listened' to children's bodies, actions, preferences and mark making. By listening in such an active way – not only to the relatively simple utterances of these two-year-olds but also to their preferences – for particular materials, used in particular ways in particular spaces, the adults close to them were about to create a schematic pedagogy (Atherton and Nutbrown 2016) which supported each child's questioning.

The first four chapters in the book set out aspects of theory, research and policy that underpin and interweaves early childhood education. We see young children as important and central 'actors' in their own social worlds of nursery and home, and as co-constructors of knowledge in those worlds. We set out the particular approach for reflecting on Julies' observations of the four children – schematic theory – whereby we attempt to make our own sense of the meanings beneath the children's explorations. In so doing we can see that far from 'flitting' from one activity to another, they are in fact 'fitting' (Athey 2007) together different experiences to create a coherent 'thread' which connects their learning enterprises. What Athey called 'fitting not flitting' and what Van Wijk (2008: 2) calls 'wondering not wandering' are important underpinnings to schematic pedagogy which, as we shall see, is not always an easy fit with some early years policies.

All this comes together in the children's own intrinsically personal explorations that are born of the cultural nuances of each of their family lives and the environment for exploration in their nursery.

It is the opening up and understanding of the cultures of family and of learning that can lead us to real and effective collaborations between young children, their parents and their practitioners for, as Athey (1990: 66) said, 'Nothing gets under a parents skin more quickly and more permanently than the illumination of his or her own child's behaviour. The effect of participation can be profound.'

1

Young Children as Actors in
Their Own Learning

In the context of recent research into the learning and development of young children, this chapter will review the criticality of children's physical, social and emotional development within their first few years of life. In this book, young children are considered as co-constructors of their own knowledge who, even at such young age, already have their own 'worthwhile and insightful understanding of the world' (Janzen 2008: 292).

It is crucial that the interconnected nature of all aspects of young children's development is recognized. During the first three years of life, learning and development are rapid and all aspects of their body and being are growing. These are the years when children's emotions are forming, when children gain control over their bodies, when their brains are developing rapidly and when their vocabulary expands daily. All this makes it imperative that those who work with our youngest children have a deep knowledge of how children learn and develop. This chapter gives a brief exploration of some underpinning theories and recent research relating to young children's development and learning and seeks to highlight the 'preciousness' (Atherton and Nutbrown 2013: 6) and criticality of a child's experiences in their second year of life and learning.

The criticality of early experiences

Fundamental to all human development is the need to feel safe and emotionally secure, and for young children their need for security within their environment is essential to their well-being and development (Clare 2012; Gerhardt 2004). In this context, emotional security is synonymous with attachment. Bowlby (1997: 195) defines attachment as 'seeking and maintaining proximity to another individual' and modern attachment theory stresses the importance of children developing multiple close attachments where positive and close relationships are an essential part of human existence (Cassidy and Shaver 2008; Degotardi and Pearson 2009). Page, Clare and Nutbrown (2013: 34) acknowledge that 'close, intimate and trusting relationships are essential to the well being of every one of us' and Field (2010: 7) identified that what matters to young children is loving and responsive parents who create a secure bond with their child. Hughes (2006) also suggested that, during a young child's life, the importance of love cannot be ignored:

> From a baby's point of view, if someone loves you and sees you as lovely, you feel lovely. If the closest adults are responsive, gentle and loving … he [sic] will trust that the world will give him what he [sic] needs. Without love, the baby becomes anxious and does not reach out. If the baby does not reach out, he [sic] does not touch the world and remains locked in his [sic] own world. (Hughes 2006: 7)

Such security enables the development of relationships and, consequently, the development of an attachment between the child and parents (Bowlby 1989). Within the context of a full day care setting, the importance of young children forming secure attachments cannot be underestimated. Elfer et al. (2012) conclude that, in the absence of parents, these children need the attachment of a special person, often referred to as a 'key' person.

Clare (2012) describes how, through providing a safe, secure and nurturing environment, day care settings can support children to form attachments. She gives an example from a nursery setting that encourages parents to take photographs 'of the people/things that are important to their child' (23) at home, which they also do in the nursery. The photographs are collated into a special book and kept within the child's reach, this kind of practice strengthens the view that learning for very young children is about 'self and place and space and relationships' (Page et al. 2013: 25).

Throughout this book, the importance of practitioners understanding the cruciality of attachment and a child's need to feel special is stressed. Emily's story in Chapter 7 foregrounds the importance of her relationship with her key person, and we suggest that Emily's experience of feeling special resonates with ideas of love (Hughes 2006; Page et al. 2013; Trevarthen 2012). Whilst the effect of love may not necessarily be visible, 'the baby who was looking for intimate encounters and support at birth is much more implicated in culture and more aware of friendships, and ready to profit from an imaginative preschool' (Trevarthen 2012: 6). Page et al. (2013) argue that it is 'professional love' that toddlers need in group settings in order to feel secure and 'attached' to the person who works with them. Emily's story recognizes and highlights that when considering the learning process, the importance of young children's emotional needs cannot be underestimated or ignored. The main focus of this book is to demonstrate how, with strong emotional grounding and the feeling of security, young children are better positioned for all kinds of learning explorations. When early years practitioners have a deep understanding of the development of young children's conceptual thinking, they are in a position to create exciting and stimulating learning environments for young children, and to engage in interesting and dynamic learning encounters with them. Throughout the book we offer many illustrations of the emergent patterns of young children's cognition to show how work with two-year-olds based on a schematic pedagogy can be both relevant and rewarding for the children and the practitioners.

Young children and learning

Whilst the ideas about young children's learning developed by Pestalozzi and Froebel provided early underpinnings of our thinking about the nature of childhood and of children's learning, we suggest that it was in the twentieth century that theorists were most prolific in the development of learning theories. Such theories spanned a continuum from tight control and prescriptive training of behaviour to complete freedom and autonomy of the learner, with many other contributions fitting into this continuum at different points between the two extremes (Table 1.1). For a more detailed discussion of the contribution of learning theorists to young children's learning, see Nutbrown and Clough (2013) and David, Goouch and Powell (2016).

The American psychologist Skinner (1974), working in the mid-1990s, was primarily responsible for behaviourism; a popular learning theory of the time. His approach to learning was more akin to training, which promoted a system of learning which involved a 'stimulus-response' approach in order to, in the main, modify undesirable behaviour and train towards desired behaviour. The premise behind behaviourism was based on children making an association to a stimulus that resulted in a response, but whilst this was useful during World War II when Skinner worked on a secret project to train pigeons to keep pecking a target that would hold a missile onto a target, it does not fit with a view of young children as active individuals who have agency in their

Table 1.1 From Behaviourism to Humanism – some learning theorists of the twentieth century who have contributed to understanding how young children learn

Theorist	Dates	Nationality	Key ideas
B.F. Skinner	1904–1990	American	Training Modification of behaviour
Jean Piaget	1896–1980	Swiss	Stages of development
Lev Vygotsky	1896–1934	Russian	Social nature of learning Zone of Proximal Development
Erik Erikson	1902–1994	German/ American	Stages, self-esteem, play
Donald W. Winnicott	1986–1971	English	Parent–child relationships, child psychoanalysis, transitional objects, play behaviour
Carl Rogers	1902–1987	American	Humanism, freedom, non-directive approaches, 'facilitating learning'

own learning. That said, it is not unusual for early years settings to use positive reinforcement strategies to encourage appropriate behaviour in young children – a thumbs up, a smile, a sticker all reward the appropriate 'response' a child makes to a particular 'stimulus'. In effect these are 'training' strategies to help young children learn how to behave in the social group of the setting. Some parents use such strategies at home and controversial television programmes such as *Supernanny* and *Nanny* have drawn on behaviourist learning theory to advise parents on behaviour management strategies and sleep patterning.

Working at about the same time as Skinner was Carl Rogers, American psychologist and psychotherapist who put forward an approach to education which was based on reciprocal relationships between children and between children and their teachers. He believed that human beings had it in their nature to do the very best they can. His view of freedom and non-directive approaches has underpinned some thinking about how young children learn and how their needs in the early years might be best met in order to ensure positive mental health and growth (Rogers and Freiberg 1993). The views of Skinner and Rogers could not have been much further apart, in approach and in their view of what learning meant and what was important in learning and in the person.

The twentieth century also saw the famous psychologist Piaget (1952) pioneer his work on child development, mainly from watching his own children grow and develop. Piaget (1972, 1990) put forward a view of stages of intellectual development which, amongst other things, promoted a view of the youngest children as passive and uninvolved in their own learning and unable to reach forward until they reached a particular age when they would enter into a new phase of development. Piaget observed and analysed what he considered to be egocentric behaviour in young children, believing that a goal of development was to overcome such behaviour. He saw learning as a process of moving through certain stages of cognitive development. The 'ages and stages' debate continued to be popular into the 1970s and 1980s until new views and perspectives came to the fore.

Wood (2013) explains that in contrast, Piaget's theory of cognitive development placed 'action and self directed problem solving at the heart of learning and development' (24). When young children are allowed, and actively encouraged, to explore their environment, they develop understanding from their actions.

A baby who regularly explores a treasure basket will build up knowledge of the textures and feel of the different resources, and for example, beginning to understand how to make the metal objects click together to make sounds. Through the process of discovery, the baby begins to construct an understanding of the properties of resources in the treasure basket.

Constructivists argue that through actively engaging with the environment, young children are able to construct their own learning, implying that cognition develops as a result of mental construction. Piaget's constructivist learning theory identifies the internal construction of cognitive structures or schemas. The concept of schema will be explored in detail in Chapter 2.

Wood (2013: 24) describes how Piaget's emphasis on exploration and child-centred views of learning led to the development of environments that allowed children 'to solve problems through self-chosen self-directed activities' in the belief that through engagement with these activities children would learn.

Erikson (1950), born in Germany and later taking American citizenship, also suggested that development took place in stages, determined by nature and the limits within which nurture operates. For Erikson, every stage was essential for healthy development and progression, and, physical, emotional and psychological stages of development were linked to specific experiences. Erikson focused on the impact of unmet needs on learning and the impact of this on a child's development. Much of Erikson's work supports the development of programmes in early childhood education, which foster positive self-esteem and exploratory learning through play.

Working around the same time, in England, Winnicott (1953) developed concepts such as the 'holding environment', and the 'transitional object' (something many might recognize as a child's inseparable toy or a 'comfort blanket'). Winnicott's work has helped many teachers and early childhood professionals to understand the need for some children to have their special object or blanket with them at points of transition or when stressed and distressed. Whilst some psychologists focused on children who had some difficulty in relationships or attachment, Russian psychologist Vygotsky (1986) put forward the notion of learning as a social exchange. He proposed that young children learn through interaction with other children and with adults, and gave us the 'Zone of Proximal Development' (Vygotsky 1980), which was a key contribution to understanding the role of the adult (or another – more knowledgeable – child) in children's learning. The ZPD is important where children are in groups or in a one to one situation at home or in a group setting. Vygotsky wrote that 'human learning presupposes a specific social nature and a process by which children grow into the intellectual life of those around them' (1980: 88). For Vygotsky learning was social, with a naive learner gaining from being alongside and supported by a more experienced learner.

Vygotsky's work added a further dimension to Piaget's explanations of children's learning by underlining the important and vital role of 'others' in helping children to learn. In contrast to Piaget, the cultural context is fundamental to Vygotsky's (1978: 46) work, which recognizes the 'use of tools and human speech' as 'two fundamental cultural forms of behaviour that arise in infancy'.

Vygotsky (1978) considered that children learn through social interactions and involvement in a social context. That is to say that, what occurs on the social plane is internalized and becomes part of a child's own thinking, for Vygotsky 'what a child can do in co-operation today he [*sic*] can do alone tomorrow' and he considered 'imitation as indispensable' whether 'in learning to speak' or 'school subjects' (1986: 188), recognizing that in order 'to imitate, it is necessary to possess the means of stepping from something one knows to something new' (187). Vygotsky's work identifies the need for a more proficient 'other', a view supported by Nutbrown (2013) and Wood (2013), who reiterate the need for children's learning needs to be supported with both suitable environments and appropriate adult support.

This book demonstrates how knowledge of schema theory can be used by practitioners to support them in becoming 'effective pedagogical leaders who understand the learning and development needs of young children' (Nutbrown 2013: 1), facilitating and positioning practitioners to understand, value and respect young children as the 'co-constructer of knowledge, identity and culture' (Janzen 2008: 291).

In recent years, neuroscientific studies have led to an enhanced knowledge and greater appreciation of the importance of brain development in the first few years of life. Such studies have usefully informed working practices with young children, largely by confirming that established good practice is effective. Clarifying the links between young children's experiences and their cognitive development, Field (2010) acknowledges the importance of healthy brain development in young children. In so doing he draws attention to a direct relationship between the quality of experiences a young child gains and the growth and development of the brain. The first three years of life are often referred to as a critical period for developing rich and complex connections. Gopnik, Meltzoff and Kuhl (1999) confirm that sensory play experiences support the connections made in the brain. As babies grasp and move their arms, muscular strength develops and the positive sensory feedback from this play encourages the child to repeat it. 'Such sensory motor experiences are considered crucial for early development' (Corbetta and Snapp-Childs 2009: 44) and the repeated actions are said to strengthen the neural pathways, signifying that the 'experience of being alive in the world grows from the sensation of body movement' (Trevarthen 2012: 5). Everything a baby hears, sees, tastes, smells and touches provides a varied and wide-ranging sensory experience that contributes to the essential development of the neural connections.

Of course, when thinking about young children's cognitive development, it is important that we do not simply focus on young children's brains, their whole bodies are important in their learning, as are their emotions. Young children are physical beings, and Gardner's (1984: 208) theory of multiple forms of intelligence stresses the role of the body. He dismisses a 'divorce between the mental and the physical' as the assumption that motor activity is subservient to thought, instead promoting the view that what we do with our bodies is equal to language and the logic of the mind, providing a foundation for Johnson's (1987) belief that from the embodied experiences of physically manipulating objects, bodily movement, perception and learning can be shaped. This is a view shared and illustrated in Part Two of this book through the individual stories of Abby, Hannah, Emily and George. If we are to deepen our understanding of young children's learning, we must do so by observing them, reflecting on what we see and learning from children themselves.

Building on Piaget's (1959) idea of thought as internalized action, Greenland (2000) developed the idea of 'body thinking', describing 'mental thoughts that arrive by way of words or pictures and body thoughts that arrive by way of wiggles and jiggles' (8). This emphasizes that it is only through recognizing and listening to the direct perceptions that come through the body that we are fully able to recognize how young children learn.

As children grow it is important to remain mindful of the physicality of learning as well as the 'invisible' workings of the mind. We must see young children as a whole – body, mind and soul, if we are fully to recognize and understand their developing cognition. Importantly, Matthews (2010) highlights the perceptions that young children gain through what he calls 'meaningless actions – twirling, running, jumping up and down, shouting, singing, apparently aimlessly messing around with objects', he suggests that such actions can be linked to children's drawing and painting (3). Nutbrown (2011) also reasons that these movements and marks are essential underpinnings to written language. Matthew maintains that 'action representation has rarely been described and its relationship to the development of drawing [and painting] is yet to be fully understood' (2010: 24). However, he states:

> The very notion that drawing might be merely physical is to this writer, wrong headed anyway. Painting, like any other activity, is multi modal, involving kinaesthetic, proprioceptor, and haptic, as well as visual information. The traditional division between what is considered sensorimotor and the mental activity is an artificial and meaningless one. (Matthews 2010: 19)

Examples of how young children represent their forms of thought as figurative marks are explored in Chapters 5 and 8.

This chapter has highlighted the importance and interconnected nature of all aspects of young children's development. We have highlighted the importance of the first three years of life, when learning and development are rapid and all aspects of young children's bodies are growing. This makes it imperative that those who work with our youngest children have a deep knowledge of how children learn and develop.

The role of physical action within young children's learning still lacks due recognition, and remains a somewhat undervalued subject. This book illustrates how a schematic pedagogy can provide practitioners and parents with knowledge and tools that they can use further to understand and meet the needs of children. Providing a detailed analysis of four young children's schematic endeavours pursued over sixteen weeks, Part Two of the book gives clear illustrations of how two-year-old children use their senses and actions to develop and extend their thinking.

2

Schematic Theory

A variety of learning theories that were developed and became popular during the twentieth century were introduced in Chapter 1. This chapter will trace the origins of schema theory to offer an understanding of how schemas can be nourished through children's embodied, physical experiences with the environment and with others (both adults and children) at home and in group settings. This chapter provides an overview of the definitions and characteristics of schema and how young children's schemas can support their mark making and their thinking.

Through her groundbreaking Froebel Early Education Project (1973–1978), Athey (1990) made a major contribution to the knowledge and understanding of how young children learn. Having applied Piaget's theory of schema to children aged between two and five years, Athey's work made it possible for thousands of practitioners, in many parts of the world, to gain a more insightful perspective on children's thinking. Athey's interpretation and categorization of schema inspired a 'conscious and articulated pedagogy' (Whalley 2010: xii), providing a window through which the process and business of young children's learning can be viewed. Athey focused primarily on three- to five-year-olds but younger siblings were also included in the project and so her work began to shed light on the learning actions of two-year-olds. This book is underpinned by Athey's work and provides some detailed accounts of two-year-old children's patterns of thinking; their schemas.

Atherton and Nutbrown (2013: 8) consider that 'no single characterization is able to satisfy' the complexities and differing perspectives around the concept of schema, here they are referring to the deep thinking that is required to try to penetrate the patterns of action, movement and thought that are children's schemas. It is for this reason that providing a simple definition of schema is not possible, instead various construct and views will be explored.

In tracing the origins of schema, McVee, Dunsmore and Gavelek (2005) identified the opposing views of cognitive science and cognitive psychology.

Describing how cognitive science simply considers schema as an information-processing concept carried out by an individual is a simplistic view that is not supported by the observations and discussions within this book which uncover young children's complex thinking. Cognitive psychology considers a more complex approach advocating that 'we think of them [schema] as patterns that extend beyond the knower into the social and cultural world' (McVee et al. 2005: 535).

Recognizing the relationship between 'in the head' learning and skill development through adjustments made as a result of the interpretation of messages from outside the body, Bartlet (1958) identified:

> Skilled performance must at all times submit to receptor control, and must be initiated and directed by the signals which the performer must pick up from his environment, in combination with other signals to his own body, which tell him about his own movements as he makes them (14 *sic*).

This reinforces the view that schemas develop as a result of both the embodied and mediated experiences with the world, as illustrated in this book. Accepting this interpretation of schema implies that schema shapes both the experiences young children gain and their thinking; through involvement within the schematically underpinned experiences their thinking is enhanced. This causes us to question further how the experiences and environments young children inhabit impact on their cognitive development. How do social and cultural experiences nourish children's schemas?

Piaget and Inhelder (1969) paid great attention to the links between sensory activity and learning, naming it the sensory-motor phase, emphasizing the embodied and active nature of learning. This relates to Athey's (2007) belief that the relationship between a child's motor actions and sensory feedback is central to the learning process. Corbetta and Snapp-Child (2009) clarify that:

> By seeing and touching objects, by bringing them to the mouth, and by manipulating them, infants can learn about their physical properties, they can remember their specific characteristics, and use this newly acquired knowledge to plan future actions (44).

Atherton and Nutbrown (2013) illustrate this in their description of Annie's 'powerful discoveries' during her sensory and physical exploration of a basket and her possible thoughts 'What is this and what can I do with it? If I turn it over I can see the bottom' (97).

Piaget (1953) and Furth (1969) demonstrated that schemas develop as a result of assimilation; the progression of the 'new' into the 'familiar' with the acceptance that, in order to increase cognitive structure, every scheme of assimilation must also be accommodated. Furth (1969) suggested that people build up working cognitive theories by repeating actions, thus assimilating and accommodating new information into current models of thought. Using the sucking action of a baby to illustrate this theory, he observed how such sucking behaviours vary according to the different object and materials explored. 'There is a difference between the sucking that results in swallowing and other sucking' (Furth 1969: 45). He suggested that a baby actively incorporates new experiences into her or his existing cognitive structure, resulting in an adjustment or modification of the structure. This means that through the process of assimilation and accommodation, the cognitive structure – the schemas – become more complex and learning can be observed. In Chapter 8 we see how George's learning occurs and how more complex learning develops as his prior experiences of 'trajectory' and 'containing' schemas appear to combine to support and facilitate his new interests in 'going through a boundary'.

Defining schema, Athey (2007: 5) describes a 'pattern of repeatable actions that lead behaviour and thinking in children that exists underneath the surface features of various contents, contexts and specific experiences'. Building on Athey's definition, Nutbrown (2011) asserts that it is from these early patterns of behaviour that the foundation of young children's learning can be observed and supported, something that we seek to illustrate in this book.

Athey (2007) also recognized and acknowledged that the growth of schemas occurs through the function of assimilation and accommodation. The findings from the Froebel Early Education Project (Athey 2007) highlight the notion that children's lived learning experiences relate to different levels of functioning.

- 'Motor-level behaviour' – a stage at which a child simply performs actions with no significance attached.
- 'Symbolic functioning action' – supported by thoughts that allow symbolic representation. This involves the capacity to form mental imagery. Children use one symbol to represent another, displayed by making marks, play and speech (Athey 2007; Furth 1969).
- 'Functional dependency' – the dependent relationship between effect and actions (Athey 2007; Bruce 2005).
- 'Thought level' – allows events to be discussed and described in the absence of a concrete reminder (Athey 2007; Furth 1969).

Nutbrown (2011: 145) maintains that schemas 'sensitize' children to specific 'events and phenomena in the environment'. Such patterns in children's actions and behaviour can indicate common themes, 'fascinations' (Meade and Cubey 2008: 3) or 'consistent threads' (Nutbrown 2011: 13), thus facilitating children to determine and maintain their own intrinsic motivations through identifying elements within the environment that provide a match for such thought patterns. This resonates with Neisser's (1976: 56) belief that 'a schema is a pattern of action as well as a pattern for action'. In relation to young children this suggests a schematic motivation which positions young children as 'co-constructors of knowledge' (Janzen 2008: 291), and who are intrinsically driven to find experiences and stimuli in their environment which provide a match with their thoughts.

It is important that those who work with young children have an understanding of the multiple definitions of schemas and can form their own understanding as they gain more experience, of how to use schematic theory to support young children's learning. Athey (2007: 55) refers to such 'pieces of thought' as *forms of thought* and Nutbrown (2011: 46) likens *form of thought* to having 'persistent threads' of thinking. She explains that children have 'persistent threads of action, representation, speech and thought' that they apply to a variety of activities in order to make connections with the '*content*'. Meade (1995: 2) extends this concept depicting schemas as:

> Pieces of thoughts ... not like the pieces of a jigsaw, because they don't fit in only one place. Perhaps the best metaphor is ... like pieces of Lego which can be fitted into lots of different structures.

This concept is illustrated in Chapter 6, as Hannah is observed exploring her trajectory interest. The variety of resources in the environment allows Hannah to test her thoughts in many different ways. Just like the piece of lego, Hannah's persistent threads fit successfully into the different environmental content.

Used in this way, *content* refers to aspects and objects within the environment, with children's differing experiences supporting cognitive constructions to develop through the 'fitting of content to different schematic threads' (Nutbrown 2011: 47).

> If a child is focusing on a particular schema related to roundness, we could say the child is working on a circular schema. The *form* is roundness and the *content* can be anything that extends this form: wheels, the London Eye, rotating machinery, rolling a ball, the spinning of the planets. (Nutbrown 2011: 47)

Such threads or continuity of interests provide meaningful and significant opportunities for children to gain new ideas and a greater understanding of the world.

Nutbrown (2011) stresses the importance of nourishing young children's *forms of thought* with worthwhile and interesting *content* to maintain children's own intrinsic and natural motivations for learning. Atherton and Nutbrown (2013: 67) describe how providing two-year-old Henry with an environment that supported him to build 'bigger, higher towers' facilitated the 'practical ground work to secure Henry's later conceptual thought'. They consider such attuned intervention to be a 'professional duty for practitioners' (2013: 71). Such attuned intervention can be part of every child's daily experience and we suggest that it should be in every practitioner's repertoire understanding of what a two-year-old child's schema might look like, and to create conducive environments to support them.

Athey's 'dynamic' schemas

Athey (2007: 50) confirmed that children gain new ideas through assimilating experiences (content) to existing thoughts (form) suggesting that, through the process of assimilation and accommodation, *forms of thought* gradually coordinate leading 'to higher levels and more powerful schemas'.

Through a process of systematic observation and analysis, Athey (2007: 115) drew on the work of Piaget and her observations in the Froebel Early Education Project (1973–1978) to label and describe 'eight clearly distinguishable ... action schemas':

1. Dynamic vertical.
2. Dynamic back and forth.
3. Circular direction and rotation.
4. Going over, under or on top.
5. Going round a boundary.
6. Enveloping and containing.
7. Going through a boundary.
8. Thought.

The groundbreaking study that identified these schemas from over 6,000 observations provides a strong basis from which others interested in working with schemas can further develop the approach. Illustrating Piaget and Inhelder's (1969) understanding of embodied learning and the links between sensory activities and learning, Athey (2007) explains that, at a motor level, children who pursue a 'containing and enveloping' schema exhibit such behaviour as placing objects into containers or entering enclosed spaces themselves. Nutbrown (2011: 13) describes how 'toddlers work hard, collecting a pile of objects into the lap of their carer'. Motor level activity is further illustrated by Atherton and Nutbrown's (2013: 48, 49) example of Henry's actions in rolling a soft play cylinder and 'kicking objects along the floor' as he demonstrates his *dynamic back and forth' schema*; such examples reinforce the premise that young children's future symbolic representation occurs through the repetition of experimental actions at the motor level. Through multiple examples and illustrations like these we can see young children's emerging cognitive development resulting from their experiences at nursery and home.

Visual and physical representation

Identifying what a two-year-old child's schema looks like requires the acknowledgement and appreciation that young children's thinking can be expressed graphically and physically. Paying attention to children's mark making and to their movement can offer vital clues to their thinking.

In relation to young children, Piaget and Inhelder (1969: 64) consider drawings and pictures to represent the 'conceptual attributes' that the child is familiar with, rather than their concern for the 'visual perspective', suggesting it is the *form of thought*, the schematic interest that the child is representing rather than the content, the object of topic that 'feeds' the *form*. Of course, the mark making of many two-year-olds is not immediately recognizable in terms of any kind of representation, but the marks themselves may well offer a clue to the schemas that presently dominate their thinking. Wood and Hall (2011: 271) suggest that symbolic representation, used as a way of transforming and illustrating every day experiences, demonstrates 'children's agency – how they act in and on the world'. In her work with Henry, Atherton illustrates a relationship between Henry's dynamic action schemas and his subsequent mark making, affirming the link between *forms of thought* represented through mark making and drawing and the link from physical to graphic representation (Atherton and Nutbrown 2013). In such situations, Matthews (2010: 24) explains a possible tendency to consider 'representation as a *re*-presentation of a prior experience' rather than the 'essentially dynamic, constructive act which shapes the experience itself'. We would argue that mark making can be a 'representation' – standing for something in its self – but can also serve as a way of *re*-presenting a prior experience. Matthews stresses the importance of young children creating visual representations because when children use a mark or action to represent something they are making 'something stand for something else' (Matthews 2010: 1).

> In actions they [children] can make with their own bodies, and in actions they can perform upon objects and media, but perhaps especially with drawing and painting media, children learn how to form representations. (Matthews 2010: 1)

Whilst Matthews' (2010) work makes no specific connections to schema, one reading of his work is that it carries an implication that young children's mark making could represent their embodied threads of thought. This raises an idea that will be illustrated and explored in more detail later through identifying what two-year-old children's schemas might look like.

Matthews (2010) suggests that children's drawings follow an organized and meaningful continuum, a perspective supported by Athey's (2007) Froebel Early Education Project, in which twenty-four distinguishable marks were identified from the collection of over 5,000 observations and drawings. These were grouped into 'two criteria – straight *lines* and *curves*' (62). When analysing the marks and drawings, Athey (2007) paid great attention to the *form of thinking* illustrated within the work. She explained 'if a drawing was named "wheel" at one time, followed by "flower" it was because the child was representing those, and other objects' (66). This raises issues about the knowledge practitioners need if they are successfully to support young children's learning.

Wood and Hall (2011) conclude that 'Educators need deep understanding of children's play, and the processes that link play and drawing' (280), thus warning that within present educational and development discourse drawing can be positioned merely 'as an emergent or pre-writing skill' (269). Ring (2010) suggests that misconceptions about the role of mark making and drawing has had a detrimental effect on educational practices with young children. The use of drawing and mark making has not been given sufficient recognition as a meaning-making process. Wood and Hall (2011: 280) suggest that such a view has resulted from the 'limited educational purposes of play and drawing in curriculum policies in England where educational discourse has valued writing more highly than drawing' (Matthews 2010; Ring 2010; Wood and Hall 2011). When we think of two-year-olds, their marks are often derided as 'only scribble', lacking meaning and skill, so considerable work is needed to give due recognition to the place of the early marks children make – often initially experimental – to their learning. We might say that drawing and mark making have two essential purposes, the first (and most important) is that they are a way of making meaning for children and, in this process children rehearse and refine the marks that eventually they employ for conventionally recognizable handwriting (the second purpose). We suggest, with Athey (2007), that first marks are bodily registrations; further we can consider that marks are later *purposefully made* by children to represent or make meaning (either movements or objects or experiences or events) and finally having mastered many versions of lines, curves, angles and intersecting marks, they are in a position to employ them in conventionally recognizable writing. This is not to say that drawing is inferior to writing but rather to suggest that without drawing children cannot become naturally adept at conventional writing. Further we would argue that acquiring the skills necessary for mastering the conventions of handwriting is much better done through purposeful and self-directed mark making and drawing than through laborious and adult imposed copying and tracing of patterns imposed by adults in the hope of teaching handwriting.

Ring (2010) also identifies that the act of replacing the word 'drawing' with 'mark making' has further separated it from the spontaneous acts young children are involved in as they come to understand the world, thus appearing to portray the role of drawing 'as servants to defined curriculum goals' (Wood and Hall 2011: 280). It need not be like this, instead such activities can be identified as necessary human actions (Dissanayake 2015) upon which young children's future learning is founded. We suggest that 'mark making' and 'drawing' can be differently defined, because in drawing is implied the making of meaning, whereas in mark making we can find representation of *form* but cannot necessarily find additional meaning unless other information is available.

Wood (2013) argues that measuring and matching children's actions through a curriculum lens raises the discourse of 'play' or 'work'. It is recognized that children have different perceptions of 'play' and 'work' and as Howard et al. (2002: 3) recognized the 'play–work dichotomy', suggests that children's 'specific mind-set' (10) changes depending on their interpretation of the activity. The importance of children perceiving an activity as play 'allows the exploitation of children's natural propensity to play' (12). Such enhancing, intrinsic motivation, enthusiasm, willingness and engagement were seen in Henry where his continual exploration of dynamic vertical movements are described as reaching up, putting objects on different steps, climbing and crawling up steps, running, walking or sliding down the slide (Atherton and Nutbrown 2013). Examples of Henry's vertical and horizontal lines (mark making) are used to illustrate possible links between Henry's physical activities and his painting, suggesting that there are symbolic representations of Henry's continuous actions – his schema – which is represented figuratively with paint. This supports Matthews' (2010: 36) belief that:

> Out of the seemingly chaotic actions of the infant, there is articulated a gestural language on which symbolization will be built. Without this language in place, no further learning is possible.

Schematic pedagogy

All of this raises the issue of curriculum content for two-year-olds, which we shall discuss later, but for now we want to identify the place of pedagogy. The specific learning needs and interests of two-year-olds demands some quite particular pedagogical approaches, and from a schematic point of view such young children need a pedagogy that supports their wonder and awe, inquisitive resolve, sensory, bodily inquiry and creative expression (Atherton and Nutbrown 2016).

This view of schematic pedagogy underpins our discussions in this book:

> We suggest that a schematic pedagogy is creative, artistic, inventive, unconventional and filled with possibility. There is a determination in schematic pedagogy to pay attention to what matters to children and cultivate an approach to practice which centres the child and their particular, individual thinking concerns. Schematic pedagogy is a pedagogy of tessellation where 'fit' of ideas and approaches are core, and where the relational and physical come together. It is a place where professional adults come to know children in new ways through meticulous observation and where practice may be shaped to fit what is significant to each child. In schematic pedagogy children are partnered in their play by adults who admire what they see, knowing children to be young proficient and determined to match this with precise accompaniment. Schematic pedagogy is an accomplished approach to supporting early learning through taking time to attune to children's own significances thus yielding great riches of learning and understanding. (Atherton and Nutbrown 2016: 14)

This chapter has highlighted the complex nature of schema, yet, we need to consider what the 'significance is for practice' (Atherton and Nutbrown 2013: 10). A recognition and understanding of schemas provides an understanding of the importance, value and influence that environments and adults can have on young children's learning. A schematic pedagogy allows adults to develop and work within their deepening understanding of *how* young children learn. Knowledge of schemas enables practitioners to tune into children's *forms of thinking*, to match their language and resources to those forms so as to further support young children's thinking. Schematic theory contributes to both the skills and knowledge that practitioners need to acquire if they are to recognize young children's intrinsic learning motivations. And such deeper understanding is needed if practitioners are to value the matches made between young children's thinking and the environmental content they encounter as they actively 'co-construct their own knowledge' (Janzen 2008: 292). It is only through recognizing and understanding *forms of thinking* that practitioners will be more able to facilitate and support young children's schematic 'learning encounters' (Atherton and Nutbrown 2013: 10; Athey 2007; Nutbrown 2011).

An established link between young children's cognitive development and schemas invites new discussion of the role of play, learning and curriculum, and how early years landscapes have been shaped through recent curriculum policy development internationally.

3

Early Years Policies and Early Childhood Pedagogies

In the previous chapter we considered the origins of schema theory, to understand how schemas can be nourished through children's embodied and physical experiences at home and in group settings. We can see how different theorists contributed their insights about children's dynamic patterns of learning but a schematic pedagogy (Atherton and Nutbrown 2016) is not yet deeply embedded in present early years curriculum policies – either in the United Kingdom or elsewhere. This chapter explores the relationships between policy and pedagogy. And examines how schemas can be incorporated into early years curricula, internationally.

It is now widely accepted that the life experiences of all children regardless of age are important and influential to their future learning and life chances. Calls for early intervention in children's lives and learning (Field 2010) are based on research, which demonstrates the cruciality of the early years to children's brain development, their health and their emotional well-being. It is important therefore, that young children's early learning experiences meet their needs both at home and in group settings. Pugh (2010), Siraj-Blatchford and Manni (2008) and Wood (2013) are in agreement that in recent years an intertwining of recent research findings and government policies has directly influenced the English early years landscape. But this has not always had positive effects. Wood (2013: 45) reports that 'successive government policy' has resulted in the development of an early years curriculum and pedagogy based around prescriptive standards, goals and outcomes. This same curriculum was described by Soler and Miller (2010: 66) as an 'example of a centralised, competency-orientated curriculum … establishing national educational goals and content in advance'.

This chapter will explore the driving forces in the development of recent early years policies and curricula, highlighting the frequent warnings from research and, thinking about English policy, the discontinuities that often seem to occur between policy implementation and accepted early years pedagogy.

In reviewing some popular international approaches to early childhood education, this chapter also seeks to reveal the differing pedagogical drivers that influence how curricula and frameworks are constructed around the world. These considerations will provide an opportunity for reflection on pedagogical beliefs and values.

The early years landscape in England

Throughout the 1980s and 1990s, political interest in education focused almost entirely on raising standards of school-aged children, that is children above five years of age (Robert-Holmes 2012). And a national curriculum and national assessment system was introduced, it being believed to be the best way to raise educational standards for pupils from five to sixteen years of age. At this time the contributions of preschool children's learning experiences were not subject to national policy interest but there was a gradual turning of the tide from 1990, when the Rumbold Report *Starting with Quality* (DES 1990) and then the Royal Society of Arts Report *Start Right* (Ball 1994) both stressed the importance of quality in early years education. In 1996, the Conservative government introduced what can now be seen as the first national curriculum for three- to five-year-olds, published as guidelines but informing inspection criteria, what were called: *Desirable Outcomes for Children's Learning on Entering Compulsory Education* (SCAA 1996), which heralded national assessment of children before the statutory age of schooling and baseline assessment was introduced for the first time, a year later in 1997. Since this time education for three- to five-year-olds has been under the spotlight, but it is only in the last decade that England has really seen real political interest in children under three.

This interest in the education of children under five is echoed, with different responses and actions around the world, with considerable interest in the experiences of children before school, often in kindergarten. In the United States particular concerns have been raised about excessive stress on 'early academics'. In Australia a nationally agreed framework – Being, Belonging, Becoming (COAG 2009) – brought interest in young children's learning to the fore and resulted in the first national framework for early learning. In New Zealand the now well-known *Te Whāriki* (Carr and May 2000) has attracted international attention and enjoyed widespread take-up in the country.

The longitudinal DfE-funded Effective Provision of Preschool Education (EPPE) project (Sylva et al. 2004: i) investigated 'the effect of preschool education and care on children's development' in the United Kingdom. The findings from the EPPE project (Sylva et al. 2004) have been 'extremely influential' (Siraj-Blatchford and Manni 2008: 24), impacting on future government policy initiatives. The project recruited and tracked 3,000 three-year-old children between 1997 and 2003, to explore five questions:

1. What is the impact of preschool on children's intellectual and social/ behavioural development?
2. Are some preschools more effective than others in promoting children's development?
3. What are the characteristics of an effective preschool setting?
4. What is the impact of the home and child history on children's development?
5. Do the effects of preschool continue through Key Stage 1?

Follow-up studies have traced some of the original cohort into their sixteenth year.

In 2000 the introduction of the statutory Curriculum Guidance for the Foundation Stage (CGFS) (QCA 2000) marked a fundamental shift in political interest in the early years (Duffy 2010). Though still 'guidance', such policy development was felt by some to indicate the value and importance of the early years, not just within educational achievement in England, but as a contributing factor to children's and young peoples' holistic and life-long achievement (Abbot and Langston 2006). However, looking back and with the benefit of hindsight, we can see the gradual narrowing and 'schoolification' of political interest in early childhood education for two reasons: (i) to encourage women to return to work (thus reducing the government's benefit bill) and (ii) to address issues of underachievement on leaving school and make young people better equipped themselves to join the workforce. The development of political interest in early childhood education has run hand in hand with successive government's concerns to address concerns about the low GCSE achievement levels of some young people leaving school.

The introduction of what we might describe as the first national curriculum for three- to five-year-olds marked a further political shift, as the interest in early years education began widening from a single interest in raising standards to include an anti-poverty agenda. Described by Pugh (2010: 5) as 'two parallel forces', policy strategies seemed to be realigned taking a new direction and moving from a singular approach focusing on raising standards, to a more holistic approach focusing on wider aspects of young children's lives. Findings from the EPPE project (Sylva et al. 2004) identified and highlighted the important developmental benefits young children gain from participating in high-quality preschool education:

> Pre-school experience, compared to none, enhances all-round development in children … an earlier start (under age 3 years) is related to better intellectual development … Disadvantaged children benefit significantly from good quality pre-school experiences, especially where they are with a mixture of children from different social backgrounds. (Sylva et al. 2004: ii)

Recognizing the need to support and provide guidance for practitioners working with the youngest of children *Birth to Three Matters: A Framework to Support Children in Their Earliest Years* (DfES) (BTTM) was introduced in 2002. The BTTM guidance material was underpinned by principles and organized into four aspects: a strong child; a skilful communicator; a competent learner and a healthy child. Pugh (2010) and Duffy (2010) described how practitioners initially welcomed such support and direction. However, in contrast, the Office for Standards in Education (Ofsted) used the guidance as a way to measure settings against their ability to support children to achieve the stated outcomes. For the first time 'inspectors were asked to make specific judgements about provision and outcomes for babies and toddlers' (Page et al. 2013: 60). Whilst the framework did not use the word 'curriculum', for practitioners it quickly began to feel like one.

With regard to policy development, the government's desire to reduce poverty, coupled with the research findings from the EPPE project (Sylva et al. 2004), proved to be an effective combination and driving force, signalling a further increase in policy and services for young children (Moss 2010; Pugh 2010; Robert-Holmes 2012; Taggart 2010). Introduced in 2004, the *Every Child Matters* (ECM) (DfES 2004) agenda emphasized the expectation that every child should have a chance to fulfil his or her potential. Intending to achieve this aim through reducing levels of education failure, the ECM agenda (DfES 2004) was critically described as 'a response to a crisis' (Athey 2007: 23). Athey believed the legislation was about reducing negatives through a policy aimed exclusively at a particular fraction of the population.

> The features that are being expressed by people in power are their hopes that the new legislations will reduce the numbers of children who experience education

failure, engage in offending or suffer antisocial behaviour, suffer from ill health, or become teenage parents. (Athey 2007: 23)

Athey (2007: 23) suggested that such policy was one of 'positive discrimination in favour of (so called) deprived people in deprived neighbourhoods'. Maintaining her belief in an alternative approach, Athey (2007: 23) stated there was a mismatch between policy and pedagogy, and continued to argue that policy focus needed to be about improving professionals' understanding of the process of how learning occurs. Moss (2010: 8) also cautioned that, despite the ECM policy (DfES 2004), attention to early years education in 2010 remained 'inadequate', suggesting its major role was still about 'readiness for school,' (academic achievement) and not the pedagogical approach of developing a deeper understanding of young children. Both Athey (2007) and Moss (2010) were of the view that future policy direction should be directed towards gaining a greater understanding of *how* children learn.

Political convictions to improve outcomes for young children continued to be the underpinning driving force (DfES 2004), paving the way for bringing together requirements for practice in 'education' and 'care' providers through the merging of the non-statutory Birth to Three Matters guidance (DfES 2002), the Curriculum Guidance for the Foundation Stage (CGFS) (QCA 2000) and the National Standards for Day Care (DfES 2003). These amalgamations instigated the emergence of the Early Years Foundation Stage (EYFS) (DfES 2007), which for the first time meant that there was a policy recognition that education began at birth and that care and education should be contiguous.

The initial version of the Early Years Foundation Stage (EYFS) (DfES 2007) was introduced in 2007, becoming statutory in September 2008. Described by Robert-Holmes (2012: 31) as 'a play-based and developmentally appropriate curriculum', the EYFS framework was also seen by some as a possible way to deliver a 'broad and long-term vision of an integrated approach to services' for young children and their families, thus strengthening the vision of a 'multifaceted' 'top down' approach to change within early years, brought about through the 'implementation of EPPE informed practice' (Siraj-Blatchford and Manni 2008: 33). In contrast, Rayna and Laevers (2011: 169) argued that as a result of the 'relevance' and 'insights' from recent research focusing on the under threes, it was time 'for a bottom-up movement where early years takes the lead'.

Considering the implementation of the EYFS (DfES 2007) as further evidence of the government's intention to reduce 'society's ills' through raising education standards, Athey (2007: 23) again questioned the government's intention and effort to try to raise education standards, without developing teachers' understanding of the process of young children's learning. She maintained that the central aim of education must be 'cognitive improvement' (Athey 2007: 31), a position also maintained by Tickell (2011) who identified that two years since the implementation of the EYFS in 2007 (DfES) 'less than half of the children (44 per cent) are still not considered to have reached a good level of development by the end of the year in which they turn five' (5). Similarly the Nutbrown Review (DfE 2012) argued that a well-qualified workforce which included early years teachers with Qualified Teacher Status were needed to enhance the quality of provision from birth to five. These recommendations chime well with Athey's call for the foregrounding of the role of cognition; she suggested that insufficient attention had been paid to identifying *how* children learn:

> What is needed is more information on the patterns of cognition that children bring to the educational situation … Questions on the nature of 'learning', 'knowing', 'understanding' and 'experience' are psychological and pedagogical rather than political, and are of central concern to teachers. They are also of interest to many parents during the years of child rearing. (Athey 2007: 28)

Clare (2012: 4) recognized this need in her work in early years' settings where she frequently observed practitioners who appeared more 'concerned with the care as opposed to the learning' requirements of very young children and babies. Clare (2012) describes how children under three years of age were habitually placed in environments more suited to three- and four-year-olds, thus they were unable to gain either the sensory or the movement experiences to appropriately support their development. This again highlights the need for greater understanding about what constitutes a suitable environment for young children and a fuller understanding on the part of practitioners about how children learn.

The Early Years Foundation Stage curriculum

The EYFS (DfE 2014: 5) continues to assert the notion that 'every child deserves the best possible start in life and the support that enables them to fulfil their potential'. However, the framework also outlines the standards that settings must meet to 'ensure children's school readiness' (2). This does nothing to allay concerns mentioned earlier about a lack of policy attention to research on improving attainment for young children (Athey 2007; Moss 2010). The main focus of the EYFS (DfE 2014: 5) remains 'school readiness', and stresses academic achievement above appropriate pedagogical approaches which seek to help practitioners to develop a deeper understanding and appreciation of young children's learning.

The non-statutory guidance *Development Matters in the Early Years Foundation Stage (EYFS)* (Early Education 2012), appears to support a play-based approach to learning identifying and highlighting three key characteristics of effective learning:

> *Playing and exploring* – children investigate and experience things, and 'have a go'
> *Active learning* – children concentrate and keep on trying if they encounter difficulties, and enjoy achievements; and
> *Creating and thinking critically* – children have and develop their own ideas, make links between ideas, and develop strategies for doing things. (Early Education 2012: 7)

However, there appears to be a divergence between the statutory framework that identifies relevant skills and the knowledge that will be provided for children through 'planned, purposeful play' (DfE 2014: 9) and those who argue that children can be constructors of their own learning. The former somehow implies the adult will be responsible for instigating children's play and suggests once again that young children cannot be trusted when it comes to considering *what* they need to learn. Whilst Wallerstedt and Pramling (2011) question if the true value of play can be maintained within an educational measurement system, Wood (2013) suggests that when play is viewed in the context of a statutory curriculum 'play becomes intrinsically bound with the contemporary politics of education, because it is subject to regulation and managerial processes such as target setting' (48), thus reinforcing the contemporary confusion and tensions practitioners experience regarding pedagogy and curriculum (DCSF 2009; Moyles 2010). Many practitioners feel that they must justify children's play in relation to learning goals and outcomes rather than focusing on developing their pedagogy in ways that recognize individual child's learning.

Learning from the past

In the England of the twenty-first century there still seems to remain some difficulty in determining what constitutes a suitable approach to supporting young learners, certainly in policy terms but also in relation to some observed practice (Clare 2012). Historically, and internationally, many pioneers of early childhood education understood and thoughtfully articulated the ways in which young children learn. Johann Heinrich Pestalozzi (1746–1827) and his pupil Friedrich Froebel (1782–1852) advocated a philosophy of education that was based on nature and argued that any form of instruction should build on children's own experiences. Frobel embraced the active nature of learning, believing that play was a way of releasing a child's inner nature, a view also incorporated into Margaret McMillan's own eclectic approach to early learning.

Susan Isaacs (1930) stressed the importance of providing meaningful, relevant and practical experiences in which the 'active pleasure' and 'eager curiosity' (17) of children became immersed and challenged in every young child's mind. She observed how young children's thoughts continually changed and developed, suggesting that a concrete understanding develops through investigating real-life questions – including those posed by the children themselves. Isaacs (1930) understood that children learn through 'stimulation' and 'active enquiry' (17), and that they gain such experiences through play.

Article 12 of the United Nations Convention on the Rights of the Child (UNCRC) (United Nations 1989) redefined the status of children and young people by acknowledging the social, civil, economic and political rights of all children, affirming each child (living in countries which are signatories to the UNCRC) the right to a voice in decision-making, to freedom of thought and the right to be heard in any judicial and administrative proceedings (Kellett 2010; Percy-Smith and Thomas 2010). Applied within the early years education landscape, this can be translated as seeing children as actors and active participants in their own learning process (Rosen 2010) and to having the opportunity to learn in the company of 'well educated educators' (Nutbrown 1996). A view of young children as agents in their own learning is not one reflected in the present curriculum framework, rather practitioners are required to focus on pre-specified goals that all children *must* meet through play activities which are, on the whole, controlled by adults.

Some twenty years ago David (1996) pointed out that we continue to underestimate and undermine both the power of play and the fact that young children can be responsible for leading their own learning:

> Perhaps the very idea that something so serious as learning about the world and how to live in it could be best achieved by being enjoyable, largely self directed and controlled by the learner, even when – especially when – that learner is a small child. (David 1996: 95)

With regard to the youngest of children, it seems – at least in policy circles – that pedagogical knowledge and understanding of *how* young children learn has made little progress over the last twenty years, and in some instances has suffered a backward trajectory.

The future

If lessons from history are not well heeded, perhaps we can turn to educational theory and present-day research to guide future policy.

Biesta (2009: 36) reports how recent policy attempts to raise standards in English education have created much discussion about the 'processes' of educational improvement. Within early years, this is illustrated in the attempt to raise quality through the introduction of statutory frameworks (DfE 2012; DfES 2004, 2007). In response, many (Athey 2007; Biesta 2009; Nutbrown 2011; Sylva et al. 2004) have argued that the focus needs to be directed on the issue of *what* such a process should be and *how* it can be developed. And here Athey (2007) argued that:

> Although there are exhortations from many people outside teaching for teachers to improve the quality of education they offer, there is an anomalous accompanying denigration of the role of educational theory. (27)

A key aim in this book is to recognize and illustrate schematic theory and as such foreground knowledge and understanding of *how* young children learn. In Part Two, we present narrative accounts of four two-year-old children as they go about their exploratory learning. We offer a schematic analysis and interpretation of each to illustrate *how* their cognition emerges over a period of sixteen weeks.

The importance of involving and sharing information about children's cognitive and social outcomes with parents was identified within the EPPE findings (Sylva et al. 2004). Dame Clare Tickell (2011) also highlighted the important influence a child's home has on his or her early development. Indeed it is now widely accepted (Clare 2012; DfE 2012; Page et al. 2013) that parents are a child's first educators, a notion first mooted in the Rumbold Report (DES 1990), where all involved in a child's learning – including their parents – were deemed to be an 'educator' of them. The important impact of children's home experiences and the role that their home, early years setting and culture play in young children's learning and development will be further explored in Chapter 4.

In many early years settings the priorities for children are the development of positive dispositions to learning (Dweke 1999), self-confidence and independence, with a high focus on social development. However, a central finding of the EPPE research was that the best outcomes for children are realized in settings that 'viewed cognitive and social development as complementary'. EPPE findings indicate that effective learning occurs when children are 'motivated and involved' with excellent outcomes for learning occurring when 'settings encourage children to initiate activities' (Sylva et al. 2004: ii). Accepting that learning occurs through the process of cognitive construction, the EPPE findings highlight the importance of reflexive co-construction, through adult–child interactions that occur 'when two or more individuals work together in an intellectual way to solve a problem, clarify a concept, evaluate an activity, extend a narrative etc.' (vi), the process being described as 'sustained shared thinking'. The EPPE findings concluded that freely chosen play activities provide the best opportunities for shared sustained thinking to occur.

Sylva et al. (2004) conclude that children make the best cognitive progress when engaged in activities with higher cognitive challenges, advocating engagement in literacy, mathematical and scientific concepts. Additionally, providing an environment that offers such cognitive challenge requires highly trained, skilled and knowledgeable practitioners that understand *how* young children's cognition develops.

Nutbrown (2011) reminds practitioners and policy makers that the important issue when working with young children is not to focus on the 'national policy of the day' (142) but on the 'process' of learning. Policy makers must understand that access and attendance within a preschool provision alone will not necessarily improve every child's development and future life chances. As Sylva et al. (2008) identified, it is through experiences gained in a good quality setting, with well-qualified and graduate level teachers with Qualified Teacher Status that children make the strongest gains. Having given an overview of some policy issues, the remainder of the chapter will consider the detail of some key international policies on early childhood education.

International perspectives on early childhood education

Whilst it is not possible (or necessarily desirable) to transfer curricula approaches developed in one socio-political locality directly into another, it is often the case that considering different curricula and pedagogical practices developed outside a particular and familiar geo-political space can provide an opportunity to reflect on established perspectives and practices. In this section we consider how a schematic pedagogy might align with some internationally renowned approaches to early childhood education.

Te Whariki – A woven mat for all to stand on

First published in 1996 (Ministry of Education), the *Te Whariki* curriculum framework has made a huge contribution to the field of early childhood both in New Zealand and across the world. The distinctiveness of *Te Whariki* is that it is the result of unique collaborative relationships between the indigenous people of New Zealand, the Māori and those who came to share the country as a result of the 1840 Treaty of Waitangi. The initial development of the national early childhood curriculum was conceived by the New Zealand Labour party in the late 1980s, interestingly it was 'subsequently delivered as *Te Whariki* by a National government demonstrating the depth of cross party consistency' in promoting diversity, equity and bi-culturalism for early childhood services (Ritchie and Buzzelli 2012: 12).

Drawing from the ongoing work of Margret Carr, Helen May and Tilly Reed, and after a lengthy period of consultation, *Te Whariki* was established and introduced by the Ministry of Education in 1996. The Māori term, *Te Whariki* means 'woven mat', but should be understood as a metaphor for a tapestry reflecting the integrated and holistic nature of the curriculum, worked by many hands, with multiple perspectives, cultures and approaches. There are some similar elements in everyone's 'mat' and there are also unique elements according to individual and community needs and interests.

Soler and Miller (2010: 63) explain how in developing *Te Whariki* Carr, May and Reed paid attention to recent research and literature of early childhood. Moving away from a developmental 'step model of curriculum assessed by measurable outcomes', they repositioned a recognition of the socially constructive nature of learning. May (2001) describes the psychology and learning theory in *Te Whariki* as especially influenced by Piaget, Erikson, Brofenbrenner, Vygotsky and Bruner. Instead of the traditional curriculum approach of content or activities, *Te Whariki* foregrounds a broad framework of principles desired to nurture holistic and empowering learning dispositions.

The four guiding *Te Whariki* principles are:

- *Empowerment* of the child
- *Holistic* development of children
- *Family and community* links to be strengthened
- Responsive and reciprocal *relationships*

The five strands that help children to become competent learners are:

Well-being – the health and well-being of the child is nurtured
Belonging – children and families feel they belong
Contribution – opportunities for learning are equitable
Communication – the language and symbols of children's cultures are promoted
Exploration – the child learns through active exploration in the environment

Carr and May (2000) considered that *Te Whariki* provided a curriculum that offered a child-centred, sociocultural and bio-cultural vision of the child – visualizing the 'curriculum as a complex and rich experiential process arising out of the child's interactions with their physical and social environment' (Soler and Miller 2010: 63). Introducing and exploring the connection between pedagogy and assessment, Carr and Lee (2012: 4) present the concept of 'learning stories', presenting a narrative form of assessment that makes connections between pedagogy, sociocultural learning and narrative inquiry. Basing many of her observations on her own children, Van Wijk (2008) identifies connections between Te Whariki's strands and various learning dispositions and schemas. Allowing curriculum planning to be based on children's individual interests ensures the child's active role in co-constructing knowledge and understanding is embedded from their experiences.

The Reggio Emilia approach – listening to young children

The Reggio Emilia approach to early childhood education is also based on sociocultural principles, central to the whole community, and at the centre is the conception of the child as a competent, active learner, continually building and testing theories about themselves and the world around them. Loris Malaguzzi, the inspiration behind the Reggio Emilia approach, a response to his experience of fascism during the war, wanted to nurture a society of children who could think for themselves, rather than blindly conform and obey. Working with the women of the municipality of Reggio Emilia he created an approach to early childhood education which valued rights, community and a *listening pedagogy* (Soler and Miller 2010) which paid attention to the interests of children and importantly was realized through the arts.

Reggio Emilia is not a national approach to curriculum, but a community-supported arts activity-based preschool system, often described as an 'approach' (Soler and Miller 2010). There are no imposed goals or externally prescribed standards indicating what is to be learned, as Malaguzzi believed 'these would push our schools towards teaching without learning' (Edward, Gandini and Forman 1998: 87). Such prescription is considered to inhibit children's own learning possibilities and within the Reggio Emilia infant toddler centres and preschools, learning occurs through the collaboration and dialogue between children, teachers, artists, parents and the community. Following the interest of the children, an 'emergent curriculum' develops, based on in-depth studies of concepts, ideas and interests which arise from the group. Considered as adventures, such projects can last anything from a week to a full year. Drawing from the work of the Vygotsky collaborative, group work is seen as a vital part of cognitive development within the Reggio Emilia approach. Children are encouraged to solve problems, critique ideas, negotiate with their peers and pedagogue, learn through dialogue and hypothesize as to why things happen or how challenges might be met. Throughout the learning adventures – often referred to as *projects* – the teacher's role is not to be the expert, but to be a learning collaborator – alongside the children, a teacher-researcher or an *atelierista*, who is highly trained in the visual arts to work closely with the children and teachers, to provoke, to co-construct, to listen, to observe and to to document the children's work.

It is acknowledged that children within the Reggio Emilia approach demonstrate high levels of expression. Young children are encouraged to explore their understanding of experiences through different modes of expression; words, gestures, discussion, mime, movement, drawing, painting, construction, sculpture, shadow play, drama and music: to use their 'hundred languages'. It is the construction of the child's identity, the values, the communication and the learning competences that constitutes the core of the Reggio Emilia pedagogy. The approach is summarized thus:

The Reggio Experiences, with its emphasis on parental and community involvement, its provision of a physical environment rich in stimulation for young children, its enchantment of children's creativity, its building of relationships among staff, parents and wider community, emerges from its sense of social responsibility towards its children and their families. (Hall, Horgan, Ridgway, Murphy, Cunneen and Cunningham, 2010: 30)

Experiential Education – well-being and involvement

Originally conceptualized in Flemish preschools in the late 1970s, Experiential Education initially influenced education across Belgium and the Netherlands, before spreading to other European countries including the United Kingdom, in the 1990s. Described as an educational model, its approach has been developed to work across all the educational age ranges; from preschool to adult education. In recognizing deep level learning, Experiential Education foregrounds two dimensions, the degree of emotional well-being and the level of involvement displayed by the learner (Laevers 1976).

Laevers (1994: 2) argues that children's well-being can be observed in their actions and behaviours, with children who seem at ease and confident within the situation are considered to have a good level of well-being. In order for children to display this level of well-being, Laevers (1994) explains that children's physical and emotional needs will need to have been both valued and satisfied.

The dimension of involvement can be defined as deep concentration: within this state the individual is intrinsically motivated. Laevers (2000: 24) explains that when in this state 'perceptual and cognitive functioning has an intensity which is lacking in other kinds of activities'. Involvement can be observed in young children when they are engrossed in their actions, they have an exploratory drive to seek further clarification, the urge to figure it out. Laevers (2000: 24) confirms involvement 'only occurs in the small area in which the activity matches the capabilities of the person, that is the Zone of Proximal Development'.

To remove issues of subjectivity when assessing levels of deep level learning the Leuven Involvement Scale (LIS) was developed. Recognized and used internationally, the LIS is a rating scale on which observation scores for the well-being and involvement of individual children are assigned. The analysis of children's scores forms the basis for interventions by practitioners and teachers.

Laevers (2011) suggests that the achievement of well-being and involvement is dependent on the way in which adults interact with children, identifying stimulation, sensitivity and giving autonomy as three vital key components. Experiential education endorses the use of the Adult Style Observation Schedule (ASOS) to monitor and support the adult role.

Laevers (2011: 5) defined the three components of the adult role thus:

> Stimulating interventions are open impulses that engender involvement, such as: suggesting activities to children, inviting children to communicate, asking thought-provoking questions and giving rich information. Sensitivity is evidenced in responses that witness empathic understanding of the child. Giving autonomy means: respecting the children's initiative, acknowledging their interests, giving them room for experimentation, letting them decide upon the way an activity is performed and letting them participate in the setting of rules.

Experiential Education is based on the premise that well-being and involvement are indicators of deep learning which reflects the effectiveness of the learning environment. The Experiential Education approach emphasizes the following ten action points to support well-being and involvement:

1. Rearrange the classroom to provide appealing corners or areas.
2. Check the content of the areas and make them more challenging.
3. Introduce new and unconventional materials and activities.
4. Identify children's interests and offer activities that meet these.
5. Support activities by stimulating inputs.
6. Widen the possibilities for free initiative and support them with sound agreements.
7. Improve the quality of the relations amongst children and between children and teacher(s).
8. Introduce activities that help children to explore the world of behaviour, feelings and values.
9. Identify children with emotional problems and work out sustaining interventions.
10. Identify children with developmental needs and work out interventions that engender involvement.

Once introduced, the Experiential Education indicators of quality learning can be easily interpreted and put into place by practitioners, making it an effective way to impact on practice and empower practitioners.

Pedagogy and the future

When considering a schematic pedagogical approach what can we take from our international partners? What alignment can we add? How can we fine-tune 'to create a schematic pedagogy that "fits" with children's observed persistent interests and observation?' (Atherton and Nutbrown 2016: 8).

In considering Annie's learning and development story Atherton and Nutbrown (2016: 8–11) use the following indicators: personal blooming; expressive growth; wonder and awe; inquisitive resolve; sensory, bodily inquiry; and creative expression, to recognize the possibilities a schematic pedagogy provides.

Personal blooming

Practitioners would offer a child-centred curriculum that provides rich experiences arising from children's own choices. Children, no matter their age, would be recognized as having 'worthwhile and insightful understanding of the world' (Janzen 2008: 292). A listening pedagogy that is not driven by standards and goals, but an environment that encourages interest, confidence, purposefulness and pursuit of individuals own interests. In Chapter 8 we observe George as 'meaningful knowledge building occurs' (Hedges and Cullen 2012: 925) as he relentlessly follows his schematic interests in 'going through'.

Expressive growth

Within the environment the practitioner's role is not to be the expert, but to be a learning collaborator – permitting children to spend time, to become involved and engrossed with their exploits, to problem-solve, critique, negotiate, dialogue and hypothesize. Chapter 7 depicts how Emily's key worker provides encouragement, recognizing and responding appropriately when Emily 'reveals her private thinking in her public actions' (Atherton and Nutbrown 2016: 9). Laevers (2011) identifies a link between children's levels of well-being and involvement and the way in which adults interact with children, identifying stimulation, sensitivity and giving autonomy as three vital key components.

Wonder and awe

The ability of practitioners to identify children's own constructions of reality is compared by Nutbrown (2011: 46) with 'unlocking a door, shining light on previously darkened areas, seeing anew'. Arguably children only discover such awe and wonder in the world when they have a strong implicit drive to seek further clarification, the urge to figure it out (Laevers 2000). This aligns with Abby's investigations of insideness in Chapter 5. Initially placing her head inside a plastic box (see Figure 5.2), Abby plays 'peepo'. To regain visual contact she has to physically remove the box. A few weeks later Abby selected a fabric net (Figure 5.5) to place over her head. Abby's use of the fabric net provides her with an entirely different experience, a new set of ideas to be assimilated and accommodated into her form of thinking.

Inquisitive resolve

Practitioners need to encourage and recognize how young children explore their understanding of experiences through different modes of expression.

The seemingly meaningless marks on a board (Figure 5.6) could easily be misunderstood. However, Abby's forms of thinking (her vertical trajectory interest) over sixteen weeks have manifested themselves through her actions of coming down slides, watching butterflies fall, bouncing on trampolines and pouring water. This form of 'physical thinking' (Atherton and Nutbrown 2016) should not be underestimated, whilst it is not possible to propose *exactly* what Abby's figurative marks represent. It can be assumed the figurative marks represent a form of Abby's vertical trajectory schema, a 'thread' of her thinking (Atherton and Nutbrown 2013; Athey 2007; Mead and Cubey 2008; Nutbrown 2011).

Sensory, bodily inquiry

Practitioners need to recognize that young children are physical beings. Johnson (1987) trusts that from the embodied experiences of physically manipulating objects, bodily movement and perception is shaped. It is important to remain mindful of the physicality of learning as well as the 'invisible' workings of the mind. We must see young children as a whole – body, mind and soul – if we are fully to recognize and understand their developing cognition.

Creative expression

Practitioners need to focus on the constructive nature of learning, children's ability to 'respond emotionally and intellectually to sensory experiences' (Brierley 1994: 67). In Chapter 8 we observe how George is engrossed in his exploration of the log (Figures 8.1 and 8.7), his investigations form the foundation for his future understanding. George's actions could also be considered as illustrating Piaget's (1959: 357) notion that 'thought consists of internalized and coordinating action schemas'. In placing the bucket to '*get the water*', George has demonstrated that he is able to foresee that he should be able to collect the water. His practical endeavours within the nursery and his home environment build the foundations of his understanding of the functional dependency relationship between water going in and coming out.

We close this chapter with the words of Malaguzzi because for us they unite the philosophies and approaches that come together in schematic pedagogy:

> A simple, liberating thought came to our aid, namely that things about children, and for children are only learned from children. (Gandini 1998: 51)

4

The Cultural Nuances of Families' Lives

This chapter will explore the significance and importance of children's home environments, to their learning and development, taking the premise that young children are active participants – not bystanders and observers – in their social worlds. The focus here is on how children's development and learning can be facilitated – or constrained by the cultural contexts they inhabit.

The significance of families in children's development

Findings from the EPPE project (Sylva et al. 2004, 2008) have demonstrated that whilst the impact gained from attending a preschool setting can be important, it is insufficient on its own to raise the outcome levels for children from the most disadvantaged backgrounds. Sylva, Melhuish, Sammons, Siraj-blatchford and Taggart's (2011: 110) findings suggest that the quality of the home learning environment is also a strong influencing factor in 'shaping children's development', a belief supported by Allen (2011) and Tickell (2011), who also identified clear links between life achievements and the experiences gained in the first three years of a child's life. For most children it is in their homes and with their families that they gain these first crucial experiences. Lam and Pollard (2007: 126) clarify that the cultural beliefs within each family provide children with their first social experiences. Moreover, Tickell (2011: 8) maintains that 'the most important influences on children's early development are those that come from home'.

According to Feinstein (2003), the social and economic circumstances into which children are born can have a strong determining factor on their future academic success, their physical health, their emotional health, their school attendance, their educational attainment and their later employment opportunities. Recognizing the relationship between socio-economic status and cognitive development, Field (2010) reported that children's ability profiles at three years of age is a strong predictor of their school entry profile. Springate, Atkinson, Staw, Lamont and Grayson (2008) reported that children born into lower socio-economic groups are more likely to have poor outcomes than their peers whose parents have a higher socio-economic status. Sylva et al. (2011: 119) established two key 'protective factors' that 'boost the development of children', and 'militate against the risk for children associated with low socioeconomic status'. The first being a secure, supportive and interested family and a conducive home-learning environment, the second being experiences gained from attending a high-quality early years setting. Intriguingly Field (2010: 7) states that 'later interventions to help poorly performing children can be effective but, in general, the most effective and cost-effective way to help and support young families is in the earliest years of a child's life'. In other words, in order to gain the 'strongest positive long-term effects', young children need to gain experiences from both high-quality early years settings and high-quality home learning environments (Sylva et al. 2011: 117).

Melhuish, Phan, Sylva, Siraj-Blatchford and Taggart (2008: 97) explain how, in positive home learning environments, children's development can be enhanced through not only stimulating activities but also and more importantly 'by developing the child's ability and motivation concerned with learning'. From an early age, the extent to which parents become involved in activities such as reading to their child, visiting the library, playing with letters and numbers, singing nursery rhymes and mark making 'has a significant effect on their child's educational achievements' (21). Melhuish et al.'s (2008: 106) findings suggest that 'while other family factors such as a parents' education and socio-economic status (SES) have some relevance', parental involvement in the home learning activities exerts a 'greater and long-lasting influence on children's educational attainments', thus justifying the DfE's (2011a: 21) statement that 'What parents do is more important than who they are'.

The role of family and community cultures in children's development

Making a significant contribution to the study and understanding of cultural influences within young children's environments, Brooker (2010) and Penderi and Petrogiannis (2011) refer to the 'developmental niche', suggesting it demonstrates the mediating and shaping role that culture plays in young children's development. Conceptualizing this developmental niché, Harkness and Super (1992) identified three distinct interfaces.

- *The physical and social environment* (the family and the organization of daily life).
- *Culturally regulated child-rearing practices* (parental practices of child rearing involving both education and care).
- *The psychology (beliefs) of the individual caregivers* (the caregiver's goals and priorities for the children).

They explain that parents' discrete cultural traditions and socialization practices fluidly translate across the interface, providing:

> Material from which the child abstracts the social, affective and cognitive rules of the culture, much as the rules of grammar are abstracted from the regularities of the speech environment. (Super and Harkness 1986: 552)

Regularity and repetition of the 'invisible criteria adopted' (Park and Kwon 2009: 59) in parental practices within the child's micro-environment (the home) ensures that core messages and values are emphasized and practices repeated. In Part Two of this book we shall see how home experiences regularly expose Emily and Hannah to opportunities to hear number names, with the result that, at only two years of age, both children can competently engage in counting and using number names in their play. Super and Harkness (2002: 271) state that 'it is through such cultural thematicity, ... that the environment works its most profound influence on development'. Harkness and Super (1992: 373) refer to the implicit and embedded taken-for-granted ideas, motivations, beliefs and forms of behaviour, which parents display as 'parental ethnotheories'. Pointing out parental ethnotheories and the developmental niché naturally foreground the qualities that are most valued and prized within the family.

Vygotsky's sociocultural theory (1978) also appears to provide evidence of how such experiences are both significant and influential within a child's development. Vygotsky (1978) states that:

> Every function in the child's cultural development appears twice: first on the social level and later on the individual level; first between people (intrapsychological) and then inside the child (intrapsychological). (Vygotsky 1978: 57)

As primary caregivers, parents play an important role in orchestrating children's experiences 'directly through their beliefs and behaviours and indirectly through

the network of relationships they develop within the family and wider society'
(Penderi and Petrogiannis 2011: 33). Thus, family members enculturate young
children in the earliest years by virtue of their presence in the family, and 'Children's
competence in the culturally marked areas is accelerated, whereas development
in other domains lags, if indeed it is even recognized' (Harkness and Super
1992: 389). This points to the importance of high-quality early years settings for
children whose family cultures may not maximize their holistic development
potential. All this means is that young children are more likely to acquire the
skills and knowledge that are promoted by their parents' developmental niché,
thus maintaining view that professionals must recognize the important and
influencing role that parents play within their child's development 'if children's
learning and development opportunities are to be maximized' (Nutbrown 2011:
164). Helping parents to gain recognition and understanding of schemas means
they are likely to be better placed to understand and support these elements of
their children's learning at home.

The social context of young children's learning

Vygotsky (1978) stressed the role of the social and cultural nature of learning
by identifying children as active and social learners who acquire socially
constructed concepts through interaction with their environment and with
others. Vygotsky (1978) viewed children's development and learning as
processes that occur on two planes:

> Within a general process of development, two qualitatively different lines of
> development, differing in origin, can be distinguished: the elementary processes,
> which are of biological origin, on the one hand, and the higher psychological
> functions, of sociocultural origin, on the other. The history of child behaviour is
> born from the interweaving of these two lines. (Vygotsky 1978: 46)

Utilizing Vygotsky's sociocultural theory, Rogoff (1990) introduced a third
plane, the institutional practices adopted within a *community*:

> Depending on the circumstances, both immediate and societal, as well as the
> individual characteristics of the person, appropriate development may take
> many courses. This is not to say that development is aimless. Although chance
> plays an important role in the characteristics of the circumstances and of the
> person, the activity of the individuals and their social partners has purpose.
> Development involves progress towards local goals and valued skills. (1990:
> 56–57)

Rogoff acknowledges that the acquisition of development and knowledge occurs on three interconnected planes (Rogoff 1998): the intrapersonal (child), interpersonal (social interaction) and community (contextual) plane. Edwards (2006: 239) describes the 'transformative process' that takes place, as all three planes interact through 'participation in a community activity', thus accepting the importance of early childhood experiences coupled with the positive and influential effect of high-quality experiences gained from within their families and homes. The quality and diversity of the interactions between young children and their parents will determine the quality of the learning experience, asserting 'what parents do is more important than who they are' (DfE 2011a: 21).

On child development, Cole (1998) describes a third force, suggesting that biological and environmental factors 'do not interact directly. Rather, their interaction is mediated through a third factor, culture' (1998: 14). In his explanation of the concept of culture, Cole (1998) uses a metaphor of a garden and growing crops to illustrate how the values and beliefs cultivated within one environment are shaped and influenced by other intersecting values and beliefs. Explaining that in the 'garden', it is possible to create the correct conditions to nurture seeds and promote growth. However, the 'gardener' must also be aware of other external conditions – some outside the gardener's control – surrounding the garden area, as these will also have an effect on the development of seeds and plants (1998: 15).

The notion of culture as a holistic feature within child development can be difficult to understand and visualize (Shore 2002; Super and Harkness 2002). When working with parents and young children it is important to recognize 'the diverse context of family cultures; their ethnicity, their faith, their languages, their moral frameworks, their way of parenting'. (Page et al. 2013: 155). Rather than highlighting the dynamic and fluid entity of culture, such a conceptualization (Smidt 2006: 77) highlights the differences; putting forward the idea that culture is somehow fixed or 'given' to those who are born into it. In contrast, Edwards, Knoche, Aukrust, Kumru and Kim (2005: 141) define culture as a 'complex system of common symbolic action patterns built up through everyday human social interaction'. Viewed from this standpoint, Edwards et al. (2005) infer that changing people's patterns of social interaction offers the possibility of influencing cultural practices. This in turn suggests that a programme of intervention, in which government policy (for example, DfE 2011a, 2012) aims to promote parental involvement in children's learning, can provide a means of bringing about change which could enable all children to gain the best start in life (DfES 2004). What is important here is that intervention programmes are build on sound understanding of how best to make a difference and that the focus on parental involvement supports parents in understanding *how* their children learn as well as what the foci of their learning in the earliest years might be.

The centrality of parents in their children's learning

Supporting families in children's earliest years

Despite a stated political commitment in England to provide all children with the best possible start in life by outlining future plans to put 'parents and children at the heart of services' (DfE 2011b: 2), such commitment has – in recent years – been questioned, due to continued cuts in and closures of children's centres and reductions in other family support and learning services. Despite plans to extend free early education to the most disadvantaged two-year-olds, the lack of power and quality in the workforce has threatened these plans.

The notion of placing 'parents and children at the heart of services' (DfE 2011a) echoed the views of Bronfennbrenner's (1979) ecological theory model and the theoretical approach adopted by Evangelou, Sylva, Kyriacou, Wild and Glenny (2009). Such a model can be used to illustrate the developing and intercepting cultural environments inhabited by young children and their families. This model can be visualized as a set of concentric circles (Figure 4.1), demonstrating the movement from the most intimate setting within the child's life in the centre to the more remote context beyond. Home environments and families' unique cultural practices are the innermost circle (microsystem) and we shall see in Part Two how Emily and Hannah's home learning environments influenced and directed their leaning. The next circle (mesosystem) represents the extended links outside of the home, the nursery setting, the place of worship, the parent groups and so on, that will have an impact on the child and families' experiences of culture. The following circle (exosystem) represents aspects which have a less direct influence on the child and families first-hand experiences, such as the parental work place, neighbours, community networks and finally there is the most remote circle (macrosystem), which still has an impact on the family and child's life in the form of social systems, such as the law and economic, educational and welfare policies. Placing parents at the centre of all services (DfE 2011b) highlights the influence and impact all professional agencies can achieve with parents, thus potentially identifying a new audience of professionals who need to acquire a greater insight and understanding of the pedagogical needs of two-year-old children.

Desforges and Abouchaar (2003) and Sylva et al. (2004) highlight the relationship between parental involvement and children's academic achievement, identifying that children are more likely to succeed in school if parents are actively involved in their child's learning and development. Involving parents in young children's education is not a new concept; around the world initiatives to recognize and enhance the crucial role of parents in their children's learning have been developed with many countries promoting parental involvement (if not centrality) in their children's learning. In the 1920s Margaret McMillan recognized that to improve young children's lives there was a need to also educate the parents. McMillan attempted to bring about change in children's lives through the involvement and education of parents:

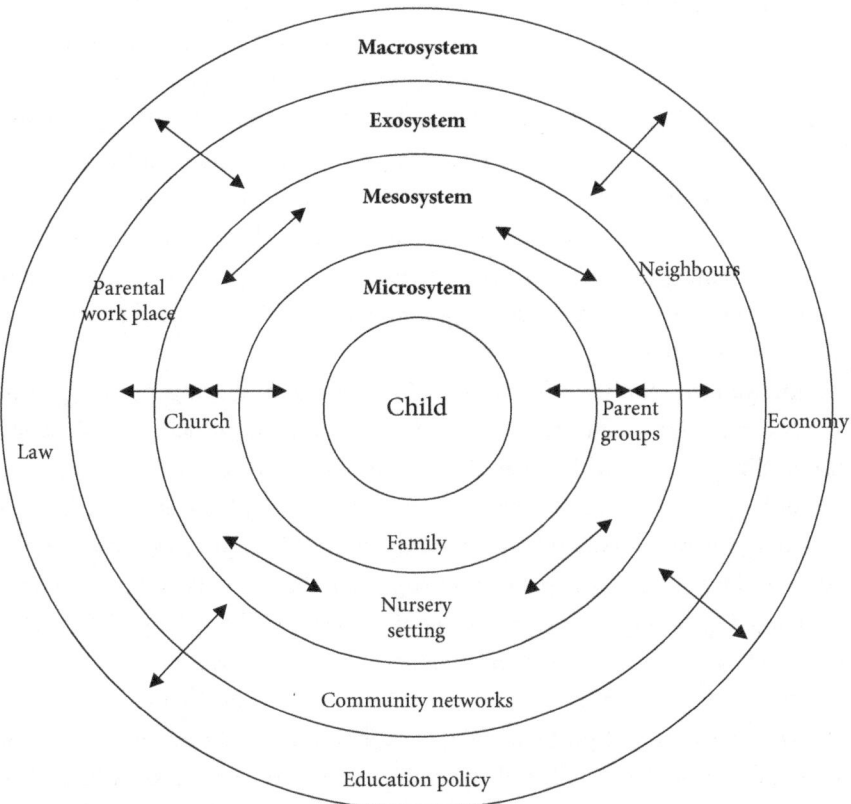

Figure 4.1 Bronfennbrenner's ecological theory

I am glad to think that many of them look upon us as friends – they bring us their troubles, show us their letters ... I'm quite sure that it is only by the personal touch that they can be helped and influenced. (McMillan 1919: 32)

One might ask how far we have come when nearly a hundred years after McMillan's work, partnership working with parents is still a matter of spasmodic and patchy realization.

The term partnership working suggests equality of relationship developed between parents and practitioners. Nutbrown (2011: 165) suggests that 'collaborative relationships' are developed through the sharing of parent's knowledge of their child together with the practitioner's professional knowledge, to piece together a unique picture of a child's learning.

Neither the importance nor the level of skill required to develop such a working relationship with parents can be underestimated (Athey 2007; Nutbrown 2013; Sylva et al. 2004). Parents are not a homogenous group; they come with many culturally constructed ideas and beliefs about child development and parenting practices, and their own personal experiences of being parented themselves. Page et al. (2013: 157) point out that 'there is no blueprint' for working with parents, and practitioners need to be able to demonstrate sensitivity, empathy and understanding. But these qualities alone are not sufficient, because effective pedagogical understanding of child development is also of the utmost importance (Atherton and Nutbrown 2013; Athey 2007; Nutbrown 2011; Sylva et al. 2008). In this book we seek to uncover children's 'conceptual knowledge' (Athey 2007: 29) which will facilitate practitioners' and parents' in gaining a greater insight and understanding of *how* their children learn.

Underpinning Nutbrown's (2011: 165) belief that 'sharing pedagogy with parents can be like opening doors to a new world', Athey (2007: 201) describes how at the start of the Froebel Early Education Project (1973–1978) there existed a 'conceptual gulf' between practitioners and parents, which was bridged by the development of 'genuine open-ended' inquiry to grow a shared understanding of children's patterns of cognition that parents and professionals developed a 'genuinely respectful' view of each other's knowledge (202). Only through viewing parents as 'capable partners' the 'true power of early childhood education' is recognized (Baum and Swick 2008: 579). Thus, it can be argued that only when parents and professionals work within a collaborative relationship, children's true achievements will be both understood and acknowledged. In 2015, the British Prime Minister David Cameron's ideas about parenting classes were viewed by some with scepticism (Ross 2016). Conversely, finding ways to realize Nutbrown's (2011: 165) vision of uniting parents and professionals together through *pedagogy* provides a different kind of possibility for future change.

To summarize, this chapter has recognized the important and influential role of parents and of the home learning environments they create for their young children to their present development and future achievements. When government policies internationally put children and families at the heart of services, the opportunity to influence children's lives through enhancing parents' knowledge, understanding and beliefs is created, and parents can positively enhance their cultural practices in their home environments to support their young children's learning and development (Meade and Podmore 2003).

We stress here the need for practitioners to be both confident and articulate in recognizing, understanding and sharing pedagogical knowledge with parents, providing the potential opportunity to narrow 'the gap between those children who are doing well and those who are not' (Pugh 2010: 13).

Wherever in the world young children live and learn, educational aims should not be solely about raising academic attainment in schools and early years settings; education must also be holistic and inextricably linked with every aspect of children's experiences and lives. It is only when education moves beyond what happens in the setting and classroom and embraces home cultures and practices that it can support the creation of collaborative relationships between parents and professionals and ultimately enhance learning.

Part Two

The Stories of Four Young Children's Schematic Explorations in their Everyday Lived Experiences

Setting the scene

The aim of this book is not simply to identify the possibility of young children's observable schematic actions, but to use a process of discovery to further knowledge and understanding of young children's schemas. Knowledge of schemas provides 'another way of looking at children', providing a 'professional language to refer to children's consistent and persistent patterns of action' (Nutbrown 2011: 24, 25).

The following four chapters present the individual stories of Abby, Hannah, Emily and George. The narratives that accompany the photographic images unfolded and grew over time. The observation process, often intense and fast moving, was also very straightforward; photographs were taken and written observations made by Julie in one nursery setting and the children's homes, only when the children were involved in self-chosen activities.

Observations were used as a way of capturing the children's everyday, lived learning experiences, and later to piece together and reconstruct these experiences and actions in relation to other adults, to their environments and the social milieu of their daily lives. Photographs can be as 'pauses in action; they hold a moment which has gone but can still be seen' (Atherton and Nutbrown 2013: 30). The photographs we present here are just a few from hundreds taken by Julie to capture the actions during self-chosen activity of the children whilst they were immersed in self-chosen play; these images provide a way of identifying and illustrating young children's schema. The use of a camera can 'impinge on the social relationships in which he or she becomes involved' (Pink 2007: 48), but Julie was careful only to use the camera when she was clear that the children were content for her to do so, and prioritized capturing the 'pauses in action' (Atherton and Nutbrown 2013: 30) over taking time to enhance image quality – thus risking spoiling or missing the moment. The use of a camera was not to capture 'professional' images (indeed many of the photographs taken were dark and grainy in quality) but to enable recall of what the children did.

An essential aspect of working with young children is the recognition and acknowledgment of existing and embedded power relationships (Dockett and Perry 2007; MacNaughton 2005). Adults cannot deny the power they hold over young children and, as Nutbrown (2010) accentuates, such power issues need to be recognized, acknowledged and addressed. Recognition of the imbalance of power between the participants prompted the exploration and eventual adoption of a feminist perspective (Aldred 1998), positioning these young children as participants in the study of their learning as 'contributing beings' (Malguzzi 1998: 52). We see them as experts, from whom we can learn, and this means that some power resides with them. This could also be assumed of the parents and key workers too, for we valued and needed their expertise.

Drawing on the works of Atherton and Nutbrown (2013), Nutbrown (2011) and Athey (2007) alongside the many works of Piaget, the photographs were interpreted and analysed over a period of time. As Pink (2007) implies, the analysis was undertaken as a continuous process of coming to understand the children's actions and their learning. The photographs and observations were grouped according to schematic themes (*form* rather than *content*). Taking time to ponder and deliberate, to look forwards and backwards to identify the schematic threads and plotlines of the individual stories (Clandinin 2006) was important and this process uncovered deep insights into the children's 'fitting' and 'wondering'. Of course, people interpret images differently (Pink 2007) depending on what they know of the context, the events depicted and their own understandings and interests. In sharing the photographs with parents, key workers and the children, deeper understanding was developed which contributed to a more shared interpretation and an enhanced shared understanding of the meanings represented in the images.

Observing the children – processes and ethics

The observations were made in Julie's nursery and in the children's own homes. She spent considerable time building up relationships and establishing an 'environment of trust' (Page et al. 2013: 46) with the families whose children are featured in this part of the book. With ten years experience as a nursery practitioner, Julie had strong relationships with all the families and children, meaning she was more of a 'research guardian' (Nutbrown 2010: 171) than a gatekeeper or *voyeur*. Recognizing and accepting the ongoing ethical responsibility to the children and their families which comes with this position was crucial.

Whilst researchers have many responsibilities regarding 'consent, anonymity, confidentiality, safety and wellbeing' (Nutbrown 2010: 17), it is important, when working with children, that we are explicit about how ethical practice extends to 'form an on going relational concept rather than a one off activity' (Warin 2011: 813). For Julie – in observing and photographing the children – ethical responsibilities went even further, she viewed children as '*other-wise* – having a different way of knowing' (Nutbrown 2010: 11) rather than 'othered' (Lahman 2008: 286), and powerless, or objectified. At all stages throughout the observation process the photographs were used to capture, identify and highlight the children's ways of knowing, illustrating their expertise in particular areas, both their conscious and perhaps unconscious *threads of thinking*. To this was added the importance of gaining the child's permission (Dockett, Einarsdottir and Perry 2009; Dockett and Perry 2007). At all times, the choice of whether or not to give informed consent is the fundamental right of every child and we cannot underestimate 'the importance of establishing an environment of trust' (Page et al. 2013: 46), where children's 'voices' are recognized and heard. On every observation occasion (whether at home or nursery) Julie made a point of seeking out the children and asking if she could join them, she would show them her camera and ask if it was '*OK*' to take pictures on that occasion. During some home visits the children asked Julie to photograph particular things – often a toy. Such occasions can be seen as opportunities to gain the child's 'assent'; when children cannot use 'adult-centric attributes' such as verbal communication, their likes and dislikes can still be observed and respected (Fargas-Malet, McSherry, Larkin and Robinson 2010: 177).

The following four chapters will present the individual stories of Abby, Hannah, Emily and George. Abby was twenty-two months old, Emily twenty-three months old, Hannah and George were both twenty-nine months old when the observations began. Whilst always taking time to gain children's assent could have meant there would be occasions when no data were collected, in reality this rarely happened, probably because the nursery environment gave multiple opportunities for children to select for themselves, and overall there were very few episodes of ethical tension experienced.

After each observation Julie took time to reflect, look through the photographs and write down her ideas, thoughts and factual explanations to further accompany the photographs. The notes included her musings; her thoughts, perceptions and questions as she began to identify and consider the forms of thought the children displayed within their daily endeavours. Julie's regular and frequent chats with key workers provided further important perspectives that have been included in the narratives, alongside parent's thoughts shared during home visits and whilst sharing the photographs.

We have drawn on the various works of Piaget (1953, 1959, 1970) and on more recent writings of Athey (2007, 1990), Atherton and Nutbrown (2013) and Nutbrown (2011) to provide a schematic interpretation of the observations. Athey's work was key to our own interpretations of the observations from a schematic viewpoint. Each narrativized observation is followed by a discussion identifying what we see as developing cognitive patterns as revealed through the children's perceptual and physical actions at nursery and home.

The children's stories

Our consideration of four young children's schematic enterprises in the nursery setting and their home environments illuminates their learning through a schematic lens and shows how the important minutiae of two-year-old children using their physicality and cognitive engagement across resources and environments to come to know and understand their lived world.

Portraying everyday experiences both at home and nursery the stories bear witness to how two-year-old children' cognitive development occurs, what Elkind (1969: 319) calls 'intelligence as adaptation to the environmental circumstances'. Reflecting across schematic stages from motor level to symbolic play the observations and discussions are used to identifying and demonstrate:

- What some two-year-old's schemas look like.
- How schemas support individual young children's thinking.
- How schemas translate and transform across different boundaries of young children's lives.
- How specific individual, and family social and cultural experiences impact and influence children's schematic development.
- How schematic behaviour contributes to young children becoming social actors in their own lives and learning.
- How the environment and pedagogy can support children's schematic explorations and development.

We have presented the observations in a narrative form using a chronological time frame, to exemplify individual children's emerging patterns of thoughts, their forms of thinking (Nutbrown 2011). The narrativized stories, photographs and conversations with the four children were collected over a sixteen-week period, as Julie, following Atherton and Nutbrown's (2013: 3) approach, attempts to 'come to know' them and gain an insight into their lives and learning. By regularly sharing the observations and photographs with parents and children's key workers, Julie could check out her interpretations and sometimes add new perspectives to the meaning she derived.

First we present and discuss Abby's schematic behaviour as she pursues her containing, enveloping and trajectory interests, suggesting how such schemas support Abby's learning as she tries to understand and make sense of the environments she inhabits. Abby's schematic behaviour is evidenced through her physical and sensory actions, her speech and her exploration of mark making.

Hannah's story follows, her motivation, persistence and involvement is evidenced as she seems systematically to fit together relevant experiences revealing her dynamic back and forth, containing and enveloping schemas.

Emily's story comes next, tracing her journey between motor level, functional dependency and possible symbolic representation (Athey 2007). This account illustrates how through 'sensitized' and 'discriminating' (Atherton and Nutbrown 2013: 50) selection of content Emily is able to transform materials to better fit her developing *forms of thought* through the use of dynamic back and forth, containing, enveloping and transporting schemas.

Finally we tell George's story, which portrays how through the coordination and amalgamation of his dynamic trajectory, containing and enveloping schemas, he is able to come to know the world at a new, higher, level. The observations exemplify George's motor level, functional dependency and symbolic play experiences (Athey 2007).

The four children's stories are followed by our final chapter, which reflects on schematic theory, schematic pedagogy and the children's narratives and considers how curricula which recognize, understand and value two-year-old children's schematic learning can be developed and enhanced.

The environment

Spending time with two-year-old children allowed Julie to recognize their capability, resilience and cognition as they attempted to test their hypothesis and understanding of the world around them. Julie has attempted to develop indoor and outdoor provision to reflect and value the children as 'knowers' and 'constructors' of their own knowledge (Janzen 2008; Malguzzi 1998).

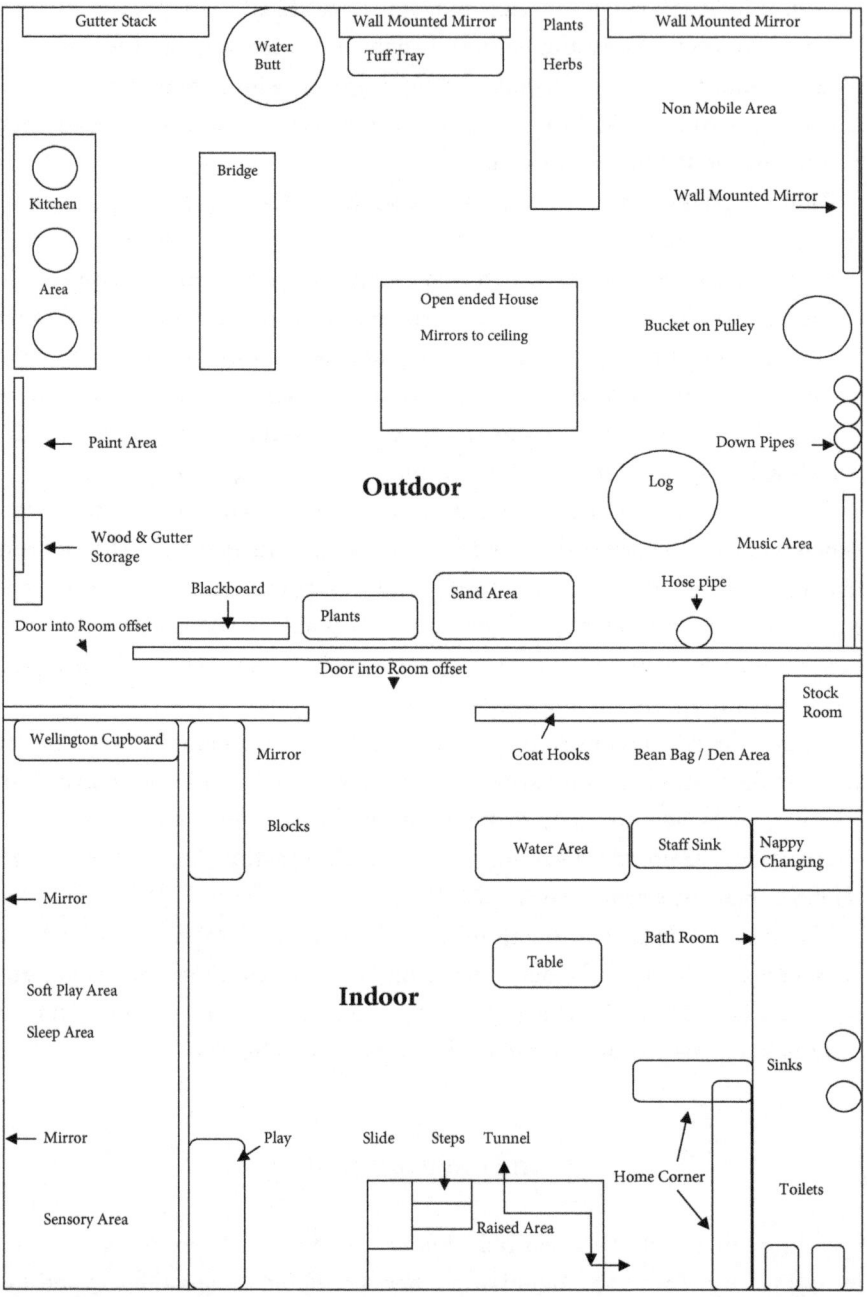

Figure P.1 Plan of the indoor and outdoor environment

Figure P.1 shows the organization of the core provision for indoors and outdoors within the Tweeny room (two-year-olds' room). Once settled into the nursery routine, children are encouraged and supported to make independent choices to follow their own interests and fascinations both indoors and outdoors. At all times the resources within the core provision areas are freely available and provide open-ended learning opportunities. For example, the raised platform area empowers children to explore the up and down feeling of the steps and the slide, standing on the raised platform offers a different view of the world, it also provides opportunity to explore the vertical trajectory movement of balls or such resources as they travel and fall from the raised platform. We see in Chapter 6 (Figure 6.1) how the guttering and the balls provide Hannah with a new experience and an opportunity to extend her learning on this occasion.

Core provision areas are enhanced to reflect individual children's specific interests, for example the raised platform can be concealed with fabric to provide an enclosed snug space, or the addition of dinosaurs or trains if we have particular children who enjoy using these within their play.

5

Containing and Dynamic Vertical Trajectory Schemas: Abby's Story

Background

Abby was just twenty-two months old at the start of these observation. She lives at home with her parents and elder sister, who previously had also attended nursery but has now moved on to the local primary school. Abby attends nursery for three full days each week, she had just made the transition from the baby room to the Tweeny room which is the base for the two-year-olds.

On arrival at nursery each morning Abby appeared content and eager, she quickly busied herself in a range of different explorations and activities. Portraying a confidence and determination as she purposefully engaged in her chosen business.

Exploration with play dough: Appearing and disappearing (24th April; twenty-two months)

When I first entered the Tweeny room this morning there were three children indoors. Abby was alone at the play dough table, initially she did not notice me. Her whole focus and concentration appeared to be directed towards the play dough. It took several minutes before she looked up and around the room; she caught my eye and smiled at me, but did not move from the play dough activity. I took this as my cue, Abby was acknowledging and accepting my presence in the nursery room (Atherton and Nutbrown 2013). I moved a little closer and continued to observe her actions.

She appeared to be fully involved in the task; Abby was using both her hands moulding and pummelling a large piece of play dough.

Abby selected two metal shape cutters, as I continued to watch I realized that she was not using the play dough and cutters in the traditional manner to make shapes, but instead pushing the metal shape cutters into the play dough, she was enfolding the shape cutters in play dough.

It did not seem to be an easy task to her – to push the metal templates into the centre of the play dough required such force that she had to use both hands and stand on her tiptoes. Abby was able to make the metal templates disappear from view. She seemed very engrossed in this task. Other children came to the table, but she did not seem to notice them – so focused was she on what she was doing. She successfully managed to hide two shape cutters in the play dough. Seeming satisfied with her hiding activity, Abby broke off two further pieces of play dough from the large piece in the centre of the table. Holding a small piece of play dough in each palm, Abby closed her grip, squeezing together her fingers she closed her hand around the play dough. Abby kept watching her hand, closing her fingers around the play dough meant she could no longer see the play dough. This action had made the play dough disappear from her view. Opening her fingers, the play dough once again reveals itself to her. Abby repeated this several times – seemingly testing out an idea about seeing and disappearing. To see the play dough she opened her fingers, to make it disappear from view she closed her fingers around the play dough. Each time she reopened her fingers and looked at the play dough, she smiled.

Later that same morning I also observed Abby placing pieces of play dough inside cups, jugs and a wicker basket, making the play dough disappear and reappear in different ways.

Abby seemed excited and pleased that she could make the play dough appear and disappear. This caused me to wonder, if she could not see it with her own eyes, could she still picture it in her own mind, in her thoughts? Each time it reappeared, did it remain the same? Did she smile because she was confirming her own newly formed theory that the play dough would still be there when she opened her hand or took of a lid to see it again.

Discussion

Athey (2007: 28) suggests that more information is needed about the 'patterns of cognition that children bring to educational situations'. On this occasion Abby seems to be interested in covering and enveloping objects. Initially embedding the metal templates within the play dough, then by containing and covering the play dough within her hand, the play dough was ultimately hidden from her view. This suggests that Abby's form of thought at this time was containing and enveloping, which she explores through purposeful interactions with the play dough and accessories. Nutbrown (2011: 14) describes this as the 'content', suggesting forms of thought can be 'nourished' if supported with 'suitable content'.

At twenty-two months of age it can be assumed that Abby's interest is not in the permanence of the objects, but the actions of enclosing and containing. Athey (2007: 47) identifies Abby's age range as a period in which children move into the stage of symbolic functioning, a time that children begin to recognize the relationship between 'motor actions and the sensory or perceptual feedback' of their actions. In terms of this observation of Abby it is not possible to propose what initiated her urge to contain and envelop the metal template in play dough. This could have begun as a motor action as she used her physicality to push and pull the play dough and template.

However what can be deduced is Abby's recognition of the relationship between her actions and her visual perception. As the metal template is enveloped in the dough, it can no longer be viewed. Abby then appears to use this experience to 're-present' the experience with the play dough and her hand. As the play dough is contained and enveloped in her hand it once again is removed from her sight. It appears Abby is able to continue to nourish this 'form of thought' as she explores her conceptual investigation through further exploits with the content of the nursery environment later in the day. Such exploration and 'experiencing' according to Athey (2007: 200), is 'the stuff or content of mind'.

Athey's (2007: 47) definition of operating at a symbolic level requires not only the acknowledgement of the relationship between action and perception, but also 'internalized actions' leading to a 'transformation of either the material or persons'. When considering materials and their properties Forman (1994) identifies the different properties of different media, suggesting that some materials provide greater transformational affordances. Owing to its malleable properties, play dough is a material which offers different properties if used by a child who is interested in exploring its potential. Atherton and Nutbrown (2013) compare Athey's (2007) use of 'content' and 'match' to Forman's (1994) use of 'media and affordance'.

Abby's use of the play dough appears not to be at a symbolic level. Her actions and thoughts appear focused on the transformation of use, rather than her intention to actually transform the play dough into something else.

Observation point:

When you are watching children playing, pay particular attention to how they use the materials. Do they explore resources in unconventional ways?

Exploring with water: 'filling'
(8th May; twenty-three months old)

Abby and three other children were busy in the outdoor area wearing raincoats and Wellington boots. The children were freely making puddles then stamping in them, causing the water to splash. I used my digital camera to take photographs, which I shared with the children. After a short time Abby seemed to lose interest in the puddles and my camera, she moved to the water butt to follow her own interests.

Abby looked in the storage box for several moments before carefully selecting a cup and a plate. She proceeded to fill the cup with water. Once the cup was filled to her satisfaction and taking great care not to spill the water, Abby moved across the outdoor area to the house area. Here she placed the plate flat down onto the table and, with great concentration, poured the water on to the plate.

Figure 5.1 Submerging a hand in the water

Abby took no notice of the other children; her whole focus and concentration seemed directed towards the important task of emptying the water from the cup on to the plate.

Skilfully Abby continued pouring the water out until the plate was completely covered by the water. After pausing for a few moments Abby carefully and precisely laid the cup on its side in the centre of the plate. Although I was unable to know Abby's precise thoughts, I did wonder if she was surprised that the water did not cover the sides of the cup more fully. I think perhaps the fascination and interest came from the fact that she could still see the cup, even when it was under the water.

Next Abby placed one hand flat (palm down) onto the plate and (Figure 5.1) into the water. Abby seemed very observant spending a long time exploring and observing what had happened when she placed her hand onto the plate and into the water. Figure 5.1 illustrates the care Abby took, no splashes were made as Abby slowly submerged her hand into the water. Initially placing one hand at a time, Abby repeated this action many times. After a while Abby started to place both hands together on the plate, causing the water to spill from the plate. Abby repeated this exploration many times dutifully refilling the plate with water.

Abby's level of persistence and concentration surprised me; she had gone from laughing and playing with the other children to a noticeably deep level of interest and involvement that continued for many minutes. What was it about this activity? Previously I had observed her covering an object in play dough. Was this a continuing thread of thought? Was she continuing to explore an enveloping schema, only this time using water and her hands as opposed to the play dough? I made a note that in future observations I would look out to see if Abby covers and envelops with other materials and what materials she uses.

Discussion

Some adults may find it difficult to believe that at only twenty-three months of age a child can consciously select resources to meet her own specific preplanned criterion, her own determined interest, her 'form of thought'. Yet Bruce (2005: 65) pointed out that 'children's schemas seem to make children alert to certain events and properties of objects in the environment'. With regard to resources Nutbrown (2011: 39) highlights the importance of consistency of resources within a nursery setting: 'children can get on with the business of learning when they are not encumbered with such worries as how to find things'. Abby displayed no hesitation in her industrious endeavours; she selected her chosen resources with purposeful ease, even after I had possibly interrupted her train of thought. Abby continued to nourish her schematic interest of containing and enveloping (*form*) using the medium of water (*content*).

Forman (1994) suggested that thoughts could be influenced by the different properties of a material. Understanding that water is transparent could be a driving force within Abby's exploration. She places the cup and then her hand within the water and both remain visible, in contrast to her previous experience with the play dough. If this were the sole focus, Athey (2007) would identify the activity at a motor level. However, Abby's sustained actions, her pondering and her repeated interests indicate that she could well have a deeper, perhaps more complex understanding.

Piaget (1953) suggested that a child's schema is continually modified through the engagement of activities and the accommodation of new experiences. This suggests that children form links in their thinking between something *they do* and a *further action* which might be a consequence of their initial action. Placing the cup in the water caused the water to move and envelop the sides of the cup; placing her hand in the water also displaced the water, so covering her hand. If Abby understood this relationship it would be, according to Athey (2007: 142), a 'functionally dependent relationship'. The water covering her hands is dependent on Abby placing her hands into the water. Abby ensures that she can continue this activity by continuously refilling the plate with water. Through further practice and experience it appeared that Abby continued to test out her ideas, prove and disprove her theories of causal connection between the amount of water and her hand. The ideas being developed through Abby's own experiences highlight her as an actor in her own learning.

Observation point:

When you are observing children during play, try to identify those children who display deep levels of interest and involvement in their activities. Can you recognize links between what they are doing and their previous actions? Is there a pattern? Does there appear to be continuity in their thinking?

Making connections: 'Trajectory movements'
(15th May; twenty-three months old)

It was mid morning, Abby appeared full of beans and very energetic. She was indoors initially, and I watched as she walked and balanced across a wooden plank. To begin with she walked very slowly, using her arms stretched out to the sides to help with her balance. After a few attempts Abby was able to run along the plank, no longer needing to use her arms to balance. Abby appeared deeply involved, I reminded her to 'go steady', she smiled at me and replied 'I steady, I go steady, I not fall'.

Abby then moved to the small wooden slide, seeming to explore the different ways she could travel down – sliding on her bottom, marching down, jumping down and even coming down backwards. As Abby explored the up and down movement on the slide she continued to inform me 'I steady down, I high, I not fall... I down, down, down'.

Abby's interest in the slide persisted and I had not seen such physicality in her before. It was as if she was trying to explore how and what the different movements felt like – first the horizontal balancing movement, then the vertical drop of the slide. Perhaps the vertical movement provided greater interest, possibly explaining why she explored this through different body movements. I observed Abby's continuing actions for over twelve minutes until I had to become involved with another child, but Abby continued after I stopped watching her, so sustaining the activity and her focus for considerable time.

When I next caught up with Abby she had moved to the outdoor area, already engrossed with exploring the water from the water but.

As I observed Abby, I noticed how she took her time carefully selecting the desired resources, first a large metal bowl and a measuring jug. Filling the jug, she placed the large bowl on the floor and repeatedly poured the water from the jug into the bowl. Her involvement was so intense that she seemed not to even notice the two children who came to join in with the water play, Abby did not acknowledge or speak with them.

Initially I kept my distance, trying not to interrupt, or become involved in the play. Abby's facial expressions indicated that she was fully absorbed and fascinated with this activity. The movement and flow of water as it travelled from the jug to the bowl seemed to be the sole focus of Abby's interest. Once the jug was empty Abby quickly bent down and scooped up more water into the jug and repeated the activity. I moved closer and spoke to Abby matching my language to her actions 'the water is flowing, the water is falling... Abby is pouring the water ... the water goes down'. Abby made no response, but continued to focus on the flow of water.

I began to wonder if Abby was making links between the bodily movements she had experienced earlier in the morning. Indoors Abby had felt the vertical movement of her body going down the slide. Exploring the water outdoors provided Abby with a visual representation of the vertical trajectory she herself had experienced. Was she now able to recognize the vertical movement of the water that she was creating? I also wondered if she recognized that in adding more water to the water that was already contained within the bowl caused a second vertical movement as the water level in the bowl increased.

Abby's involvement with the activity was eventually interrupted by the lunchtime routine, however she did not seem unduly disturbed by this. Perhaps she was hungry? Or perhaps she knew that she would be able to return to her explorations after lunch.

Discussion

Athey (2007: 116) describes the interest in vertical ascents or descents as a 'dynamic vertical schema'. Abby's interest seemed to go beyond simply experiencing the descent; when on the slide she used her whole body and several different body parts as she moved to increase her perception of this movement. This resonates with the definition of schema by Johnson (1987: 19), who focuses on 'embodied patterns'. With this he infers to both bodily movements and perceptual interactions gained through meaningfully organized experiences. In other words, bodily perception and movement increase an individual's understanding of an experience. If Abby was interested in developing her own perception of 'descent', did she recognize that using a range of bodily movements would give her more information about this phenomenon? Gaining a deeper understanding through different forms of movement reinforces Neisser's suggestion (1976: 56) that 'schema is a pattern of action as well as a pattern for action'.

Neisser (1976: 55) considers perception to be an active process; if this is the case, then we can infer that Abby may well be actively choosing what she wishes to explore and that she is perceiving these experiences both visually and through the feelings the physical movements bring her. The information she gains from the environment is fitted within her schema (cognitive frame). Athey (2007) reminds us that schemas exist in a continuum from motor action to thought. This implies that, through her embodied patterns of perception, Abby has gained physical experience of a dynamic vertical schema, so it makes sense that she builds upon this knowledge to further nourish her form of thinking. In purposefully selecting the water she gains a visual perception of the trajectory of a vertical descent. Whilst it is not possible to know what Abby was thinking, we could view this as her own development of a perceptual plan to nourish her vertical trajectory interest. Atherton and Nutbrown (2013: 42) write that Athey's 'content' and 'match' are arguably similar to what Forman calls 'media' and 'affordance'. Abby appears to recognize the affordance or match of the content and media available within the nursery environment to pursue her form of thinking – a dynamic vertical trajectory. Her selection of materials to explore seems intentional rather than haphazard or opportunistic.

Athey (2007: 117) explains that 'when 2-year-olds experience a vertical ascent, such as climbing, followed by a vertical descent, such as jumping, sliding or rolling, they experience asymmetry of effort', meaning that an unreciprocal relationship is developed between ascent and descent. This observation indicated that, at the time, Abby's interest was in vertical descent – and the ascent (on the climbing frame) was only important because it enabled her to rehearse various forms of descent; it was in effect, a means to an end.

Athey (2007: 168) states that 'two-word utterances are ambiguous', but of course such 'ambiguities' decrease as 'speech increases'. Whilst Abby used language during this observation, its context is not fully understood. We can only infer that Abby's language was not intended as a social tool but as an accompaniment to her actions. As Piaget noted, language can be used to 'accompany' and 'reinforce' actions (Piaget 1959: 17), in Abby's case her language matched her bodily movements and so we can see this as a motor level representation of a vertical schema.

Observation point:

When watching children at play, as well as observing what they do, try to understand their actions in terms of them gaining perceptual understanding through their bodily exploration.

When you observe and when working alongside children who have made their own choices of materials and actions, try to recognize how children explore concepts through the use of various body parts and movements.

Toys: 'covering' (18th May; twenty-three months)

Today I visited Abby at her home. When I arrived she was waiting for me with her mum and older sister. Abby and her sister eagerly took me into their playroom, to show me where they keep their toys. The playroom is large; the toys are stored in plastic boxes that Abby and her sister can access independently.

Abby and her sister sit on the floor in the playroom to have a drink and a biscuit. I use this time to show them my digital camera, I take a picture of Abby eating a biscuit, and I share it with her, she smiles saying, 'It's Abby'. I take this as my cue that it is ok to use my camera. Abby appears happy and relaxed with my presence in her playroom. She consistently turns to look and smile at me, whilst repeating my name 'Julie here, Julie here, Julie come play'.

Independently Abby selects a box containing a variety of toy musical instruments. After removing the box from the shelf she finds space on the carpet to tip the instruments out. Abby's mum tells me she often empties the toys on to the floor, and then proceeds to play with the empty boxes.

Abby seems uninterested in playing the instruments in a traditional way, instead she sits on the floor with her legs out straight, she places the instruments on her legs. Rather than making music she uses the instruments to cover her legs. Abby spends several minutes placing the instruments on her legs before she wiggles her legs as the instruments fall away from her legs, Abby's legs are revealed and once again in full view. During my visit I see Abby repeating these actions with a variety of toys available to her in the playroom.

Selecting a jigsaw puzzle, she once again finds a space on the floor and sits down with her legs stretched straight out in front. She opens the jigsaw box and tips all the pieces over her legs. Abby then wiggles her legs around so the pieces fall between each leg. It reminds me of how she enveloped her hands in water at nursery. Is Abby using her legs and toys to explore her enveloping interest? When she tips the toys over her legs – does this make her legs disappear from view? Can she still see the toys, but not her legs, do her legs 'reappear' to her when she shakes the toys away?

Abby's attention soon turns to the empty toy box. She seems to enjoy playing a game of peepo with the box, lifting it up and down:

I play along with Abbey and say 'I can see you, I can see Abby – oh where has Abby gone? Oh, you are inside the box?'

Putting the box over her head (Figure 5.2) Abby begins to walk around the playroom:

Abby: See me, see me, see Abby.

Julie: No, I can't see Abby, where is she?

Figure 5.2 Inside the box

Abby laughs and giggles, seeming to enjoy this game. During my visit she frequently placed the toy box over her head as illustrated in Figure 5.2.

From the fun of the 'peepo' game Abby's attention quickly changes, as her concentration and attention moves to the task of containing her snuggle cloth inside her small pink shopping bag. It seems to be a rather tricky job. Abby has to hold the pink bag in her right hand and push the cloth in with left hand. Her facial expressions demonstrate the great level of concentration and effort required.

It takes several attempts and Abby's full attention to get the snuggle cloth fully inside the small pink bag. Once the cloth is completely hidden in the bag, rather than admiring her work, Abby immediately pulls the snuggle cloth straight out again.

Whilst it takes several moments and a great amount of concentration to contain the cloth within the bag, it takes only seconds to remove and free it from the inside of the bag. Abby has found a way to make her cloth disappear and reappear. Abby's facial expressions imply that being able to make the cloth reappear provides her with as much satisfaction as mastering the difficulty of fitting and hiding the cloth within the bag. We could say that the act of hiding the cloth is done so that she can pull it out again.

Viewed from a schematic lens the activities of playing peepo and hiding the cloth in the bag have a connection, these two activities imply a containing interest.

However it seems Abby has a further interest, initially in containing herself, her head (Figure 5.2) inside the plastic box, and holding the box over her head and eyes meant Abby could no longer see me. Only through lifting the box up over her eyes did I once again became visible. Abby is possibly using the toy box and her interest in containing to further explore the concept of appearance and disappearance, or hiding and revealing. The containing and enveloping schema is the form of thorough and hiding and revealing is the conceptual content that she is exploring through the pursuit of her schematic interest. Did Abby deliberately extend the hiding and revealing concept to explore making the cloth appear and disappear? Did she realize when she contained the cloth inside the bag she would no longer be able to see it? Did she know that to make the cloth reappear she had to pull it from inside the bag?

Discussion

Ten days earlier in the month (8th May) Abby had been observed in nursery enveloping and containing with play dough and water. On this occasion the relationship between the ability to cover her hand and the quantity of water were acknowledged and recognized. It seems that through further practice and experiences at home Abby continues to explore her personal theories of causal connection between *content* and her *form* of thinking. Nutbrown (2011: 46) verifies, 'children's persistent threads ... involve children [in] creating their own continuities ... Viewed in this way, schemas can be considered at the core of children's developing minds'.

Piaget and Inhelder (1969) identified a child's ability to move freely in thought, which develops gradually and slowly as the child depends less on action and perception and draws from their thoughts. An example of this is the child's ability to see events happening outside of themselves. Piaget and Inhelder (1969) explored the development of perspectives of space. Initially children are fixed within their own perspective, unable to manipulate their thoughts to consider other viewpoints. Believing her perspective is the only perspective, Abby's experience with the red box demonstrates her inability at this time to manipulate her thoughts. Her use of language demonstrates her understanding of being *in* the box. With her head and her eyes contained within the box, her visual perspective is very limited: she is unable to see me, and therefore believes I cannot see her either. At this point she is unable to manipulate her thoughts, her own mental images, away from her own position of being *in* the box. It seems that she therefore believes that if she can no longer focus on the room, no one else can. Nutbrown (2011: 46) corroborates that within 'apparently unconnected activity [children] sometimes find (and understand) important cognitive links'. Whilst it is not possible fully to perceive Abby's thinking, it is possible that the *disappearance* of the snuggle cloth inside the pink shopping bag further confirms Abby's own theories of how things work in the world; her theory which we can express as 'objects contained inside materials can no longer be visually viewed' is tested and retested through her various actions which are stimulated by a containing and enveloping schema.

Observation point:

Sharing with parents: When you speak with young children's parents consider asking what repeated actions and explorations children do at home. How can information which parents share be used to learn more about what schematic interests children are pursuing? How are these recognized by parents? What concepts are being explored as children pursue their schemas?

Water and toys: 'Symbolic thoughts' (30th May; twenty-four months)

Figure 5.3 The movement of the water

Abby is in the outdoor area, using water from the water butt to fill a selection of cups and bowls (Figure 5.3). I watched with great interest as Abby repeatedly tipped the water from the cup to the bowl. She seemed very engrossed in her endeavours. Figure 5.3 illustrates Abby's concentration and focus on watching the movement of the water from the cup to the bowl. I smiled and said 'hello', but Abby did not notice me this morning. Instead all her efforts were focused on tipping water from the cup to the bowl. Abby eventually takes the cup and bowl to the playhouse area.

Figure 5.4 Filling bowls and plates

Here Abby is able to use the table as a flat surface from which she can continue her investigations. She carefully places a bowl on top a plate, before continuing to fill the bowl and plate with water. Figure 5.4 shows that Abby has found another bowl and plate set, so allowing her to repeat and compare her investigations with the water.

I wondered if perhaps it is the insideness of the containers that attracts Abby's interests today, more specifically, how the water fills the containers. When the water was used up, Abby returned to the water butt to collect more water. Abby continued to fill the bowl with water; once it was full I spoke again to Abby and said 'It's full of water'.

Abby: *More water, full ... full ...*

Julie: *Full to the top.*

Abby: *Full to the top.*

Using the table with a flat surface appeared to make it easier for Abby to accurately fill the bowl. Having the bowl on a flat surface enables Abby to completely fill it to the brim, with no spills.

Later in the morning Abby was in the sand pit, she was able to independently make sandcastles; filling pots with sand, patting the sand down, then tipping upside down to empty the sand and make the castle. Abby makes regular visits to the beach; her family has a beach hut which they use regularly throughout the year.

Whilst it is not possible to know Abby's actual thoughts I wonder if she may be remembering being on the beach with her mum and dad, being shown how to make a sandcastle. Abby appears to understand the relationship between the sand contained and compacted within the pot and the completed sand castle: the making of the sand castle is functionally dependent on filling the pot with wet sand and tipping it out.

Abby moves indoors to the home corner. Filling plates with play food. Abby piles the plate full of play food, then takes it to the sitting area and pretends to eat it, even putting it in her mouth.

Abby: *I eat ... eat all gone. (Places food in mouth.)*

Julie: *Abby having her lunch.*

Abby: *Eat pizza ... eat ... all gone. (Abby offers food to me.)*

This morning the content of Abby's endeavours look very different, whilst the form is consistent and reflects a containing and enveloping schema. Today the focus of Abby's enterprises seems to be filling and emptying containers. Her explorations have involved many aspects of a containing schema, containing water, containing sand, followed by containing pretend food on a plate and in her mouth.

Discussion

Sensitive, tuned-in and well-informed adults and a suitably rich environment (Atherton and Nutbrown 2013; Athey 2007; Mead and Cubey 2008; Nutbrown

2011) have continued to support Abby's continued interest in containing and enveloping, to the point that she is beginning to move on from imitating; she is beginning to assimilate and accommodate real-life situations into her schematic motivations. Piaget and Inhelder (1969: 55) suggest imitation constitutes both sensory motor level and representation, suggesting imitation can take place 'in physical acts but not yet in thought'. Piaget (1950) considers imitation as an accommodation to external models, in contrast to assimilating information to meet the needs of oneself, believing intelligence to comprise equilibrium between assimilation and accommodation.

Abby's initial conversation whilst involved with the water could easily be deemed as imitation:

Julie: It's full of water.
Abby: More water, full … full.
Julie: Full to the top.
Abby: Full to the top.

It is not possible to know if the speech Abby uses comes from her own thoughts. It is a possibility that Abby is simply imitating and repeating the words. The words suggested were chosen to match Abby's actions so it may be that Abby has some appreciation of these words, so feels it is appropriate to repeat and imitate them. Abby's explorations with the sand could also be perceived in this way, Abby is repeating and imitating previous physical activities and some language.

Conversely, within the home corner it could be suggested that Abby moves to a symbolic level, assimilating 'reality to self' (Piaget and Inhelder 1969: 58), demonstrating her transition from representation of action to representation of thought. Accompanied by words (symbols) Abby's pursuit of her containing and enveloping schema lead to recreate her experiences of meal times. Abby not only recognizes the plastic resources as food but also uses them in a suitable context as real food, suggesting within her thoughts she is able to transform plastic resources which represent food, into real food, accompanied by appropriate social language to play a mealtime scenario. This symbolic play is accompanied with Abby's developing use of language that is also associated with her forms of thought (containing and enveloping), and Julie also used symbolic language to support Abby's symbolic play.

Abby: I eat … eat all gone. (Places 'food' in mouth.)
Julie: Abby having her lunch.
Abby: Eat pizza … eat … all gone. (Abby offers 'food' to me.)

Atherton and Nutbrown (2013: 64) identify how young children's language can be further supported through a 'dialogue of conceptual correspondence' that relates to their interests and understanding rather than through the use of abstract ideas such as 'castles and princesses' whilst, for example, children are using the climbing frame.

Observation point:

When observing children involved in play situations, consider focusing on what vocabulary you introduce to support children's repeated actions? Are children imitating language and actions or are they developing their own social actions and thoughts?

Containing: 'Insideness' (6th July; twenty-five months)

In contrast to my last visit to Abby's home, today Abby chooses to stay very close to her mum. I take this to mean that Abby is unsure about my presence in her home. I feel and try to respect that Abby is withholding her consent. Abby is not agreeing to be a participant in my observations at this moment in time. I try not to invade her space. I try to step back from the play until Abby feels ready to invite me in.

Time passes, Abby becomes involved in playing a game with her sister and her mum, she appears to relax, twice she catches my eye and smiles at me. When her sister asks me to take a photograph, Abby also moves into the frame. I take this as Abby's resuming of her consent to participate and allow me to become a participant in her experiences this morning.

Abby is very busy playing a game with her sister and her mum. The game involves catching plastic butterflies with a fabric fishing net as they come flying out of the elephant's trunk (battery operated toy). The fabric fishing net has a short wooden handle attached to a white fabric netting bag, the aim of the game is to catch the butterflies, and the player with the most butterflies is the winner. It is very tricky to catch the butterflies, as they are propelled up into the air very quickly by the battery operated toy.

Abby's mum provides lots of encouragement:

Mother: Can you catch them … get some Abbs … look, catch them when they come down … good girl, Abbs.

Abby seems to find it fun and amusing, she frequently chuckles and smiles.

Rather than running around like her sister to catch the butterflies, Abby sits on the floor and lets the butterflies fall on to her. She seems to enjoy collecting the butterflies that have settled on and around her. Abby seems to enjoy watching the butterflies float down to the floor. She conscientiously collects the butterflies from the floor and places them into her fabric net. Abby seems to be having real fun, playing with her mum and sister.

Abby: Look, look.

Abby: Got one … got one … some more come.

Julie: Have you got them all … Abby is your net full?

When Abby and her sister have collected all of the butterflies, they put them into the elephant's trunk and the game is ready to begin again. Abby played the game several times, each time her activity in the game continued in the same way, sitting on the floor to let the butterflies land on her, before she then placed them into her fabric net.

Abby also found another less conventional way to use the net. She was able to place her head fully inside the fabric net as shown in Figure 5.5.

Figure 5.5 Inside the fabric fishing net

Once her head was inside she called out 'Look at me, me, look at me'. Abby seemed very pleased with herself. Previously I had observed Abby place the plastic boxes over her head; today it is the toy net. I wondered if Abby realized she would be able to see through the net – of course once it was over her head she could see thorough it and so said 'Look at me …'. When playing the butterfly game she had been able to see though the net to see the butterflies inside the net, suggesting she too would be able to see – and be seen – through the net.

Since I last visited Abby at her home, a large trampoline had been set up in the garden along side a swing. Abby asked if she could go and play in the garden

Abby: I want to go on my trampoline… I go on trampoline and swing.

Abby ran outdoors into the garden, climbed through the safety net and onto the trampoline. It was obvious she had done this many times before. Abby looked very confident on the trampoline, her facial expressions displayed her enjoyment as she jumped and bounced, up and down, up and down. Next Abby showed how skilful she was at climbing onto the swing 'High mummy… high mummy… high, high… high, high' Abby shouted as her mum pushed the swing. Abby continued to play in the garden moving between the trampoline and swing for the rest of the morning.

Discussion

Gardner (1984: 129) reminds us that 'logical science and mathematics can be found in the simple actions of young children upon the physical objects in the world'. Nutbrown (2011: 46) asserts children's threads of thinking, 'connect different areas of content'. In Abby's situations such content is found within both her home and nursery environment. Her play environments provide opportunities for her continuity of thought as she matches various content to her form of thinking and include the logical science and maths that Gardner highlights.

Abby's use of the fabric net provides her with an entirely different experience, a new set of ideas to be assimilated and accommodated into her form of thinking. The ability of practitioners to identify children's own constructions of reality is described by Nutbrown (2011: 46) as being like 'unlocking a door, shining light on previously darkened areas, seeing anew'.

Abby's endeavours continue to build on her previous experiences and expertise, as Gardner (1984: 129) observes, the 'chain is long and complex, but it need not be mysterious: the roots of the highest regions of logical, mathematical, and scientific thought can be found in the simple actions of young children'. Athey (2007) would perhaps categorize Abby's exploits with the butterfly game and the net at a sensory motor level. Abby's actions serve as a reminder that 'sensory motor activity constitutes the foundation of symbolism and representation' (Piaget 1959: 283). As Athey (2007: 51) states, 'What is "known" leads to what becomes "better known"'.

Sharing with parents:

When speaking with parents, it is important to recognize the importance of finding out what children enjoy doing when not in nursery. If we can learn about children's favourite games and daily activities at home, we are in a better position to identify continuities between their homes and their setting.

Dynamic action: 'representation' (12th July; twenty-five months)

Abby is sitting with her key worker in the outdoor environment sharing a book together. It is one of Abby's favourite stories, she has listened to it many times before, and she is familiar with the story line and is able to point out the characters in the illustrations.

The story is about a cat that loves to climb up and jump down from high places, but often becomes stuck and needs rescuing. After listening to the story several times, Abby leaves her key worker, and moves across the outdoor area to the blackboard. Abby appears focused in her actions. With no hesitation she selects a piece of chalk and begins to use it to make marks on the blackboard. Abby makes many repeated vertical marks, as seen in Figure 5.6.

Each mark is formed in an identical way, Abby uses the chalk to make vertical downward marks on the blackboard.

Abby remains focused on this activity for several minutes before moving her attention to a paintbrush and water bucket that is positioned close to the blackboard. Abby proceeds to use the paintbrush and water to make further vertical downward marks on the blackboard. The marks are carefully made, always starting from the top, and similar in size (between 10 and 15 cm in length).

Although I could not see Abby's face, from the stillness of her body I understood she was absorbed and engrossed in the mark making, the amount of effort suggested it was more than a simple and random scribble. From the concentration and

Figure 5.6 Making marks

involvement displayed by Abby this does not appear to be a haphazard task, but an organized and structured activity in which she is fully involved for an extended period of time.

Abby's involvement and fascination with this activity led her to completely cover an area of the board with vertical marks, enveloping the blue chalk marks she had previously made with the water.

I cannot presume to know what she was thinking. However, as I come to know her better, I feel able to make suggestions regarding Abby's possible lines of thinking. It is possible through the experiences of sharing books Abby is beginning to understand the use of marks, pictures and symbols to represent ideas.

Could the marks on the board be Toffee the cat as he gets stuck on the tall wall during the night? Is Abby retelling the story, her favourite story? Not presuming to understand Abby's thoughts, I can however highlight the presence of a trajectory link between Toffee the cat, as he climbs down from the trees and the high walls of his back garden, and the physical and bodily experiences Abby gained from the trampoline, swing and the nursery slide. When observing Abby at the black board she appeared to have a definite purpose, causing me to consider and question the importance and meaning of the marks she made?

Discussion

Athey (2007: 78) states that 'most early marks are figurative outcomes of bodily movements'. This resonates with Atherton and Nutbrown's (2013) observation of Henry's dynamic vertical schematic activities and his subsequent mark making. Atherton and Nutbrown (2013: 74) summarize: 'he demonstrated a perceptual correspondence to *form* in his mark making using a variety of materials and tools which were synchronic with his dynamic actions'. This is suggesting that Henry was able to replay the movement patterns in his mind and represent them as figurative marks.

Abby's forms of thinking (her vertical trajectory interest) over the previous sixteen weeks have manifested themselves through her actions of coming down slides, watching butterflies fall, bouncing on trampolines and pouring water. Without more information it is not possible to propose *exactly* what Abby's figurative marks represent. Nevertheless drawing from the works of Atherton and Nutbrown (2013), Nutbrown (2011), Mead and Cubey (2008) and Athey (2007) it can be assumed the figurative marks represent a form of Abby's vertical trajectory schema, a 'thread' of her thinking. Without language from Abby we can only say that the vertical marks are a motor level representation of a vertical schema – had Abby said 'Down', or 'Toffee going down' we could have considered this a symbolic representation of the vertical schema.

Abby's spontaneous transition 'from action to graphic' representation (Athey 2007: 78) suggests further evidence of a perceptual plan, a theory, as Abby continues her schematic journey along the continuum from motor action, through graphic and symbolic levels, to thought.

Observation point:

When watching children involved in play, consider whether there are identifiable links across activities, and across time. Piecing together observations which have a connecting schema is an important way of acknowledging children's forms of thought as well as the content of their play. Finding the 'form' of thought provides strong clues to children's schematic concerns and can help to provide more fitting curriculum content for children to explore.

Final thoughts....

In this chapter we have drawn on Julie's observations of Abby to illustrate what a two-year-old child's schema looks like. Ongoing observations of Abby's self-initiated plays have led to the identification of containing, enveloping and vertical dynamic trajectory schemas. Through these observations we can see how Abby's fascinations and purposeful interactions drive her interest and subsequently support her cognitive development.

Abby was only twenty-four months old when Julie was observing her, yet she was able deliberately to select resources to further nourish her forms of thought. As Abby's journey unfolds, it affords an opportunity to witness the initiation and continuation of her own theories about how things work and what she can do with the materials she encounters. Abby, it seems, is constructing a perceptual plan that – when closely observed – provides evidence of Abby's developing 'patterns of cognition' (Athey 2007: 28), and highlights her as an actor in her own learning.

The sequence of observations provide an opportunity to examine and link together Abby's patterns of cognition, a skill Athey (2007) believes is important if we are to further understand how young children learn. Athey (2007), Nutbrown (2011) and Atherton and Nutbrown (2016) argue that such pedagogical implications should be the driving force when developing curricula for young children.

Abby's story supports Neisser's (1976: 56) belief that 'schema is a pattern of action as well as a pattern for action'. Abby's daily endeavours both at home and in the nursery provided her with constant and consistent opportunities to further explore her vertical dynamic trajectory schema. In the nursery, through her whole bodily movements Abby enhanced her personal theory (15th May) of vertical movement. Abby seemed to test and retest her theory at home on her trampoline (6th July) and so positioned herself to further develop her knowledge of up and down (particularly down) movements. Athey (2007: 78) suggested that such bodily movement can lead to early mark making, suggesting the marks provide a figurative representation. Wood and Hall (2011: 280) argue that the links between play and drawing are frequently misunderstood within educational settings, and that 'educators need deep understanding of children's play, and the processes that link play and drawing'. Whilst it is not possible to be categoric, it would seem that Abby continued exploration of her vertical bodily movements alongside other vertical dynamic trajectory exploits at home and in the nursery provided Abby with the foundations for her early drawing and mark making activities.

Julie's sixteen weeks of observations have provided a window into Abby's life and learning while at home and nursery, and has allowed a deeper understanding of Abby's cognitive patterns, her schemas. The observations powerfully identify how schema transform and translate across the boundaries of her life and how these patterns of actions drive and support her learning.

This chapter has illustrated Abby's intrinsic motivation to pursue her containing, enveloping and dynamic vertical trajectory schemas through her everyday experiences. The detailed analysis highlights and identifies the subtlety of her learning encounters as she endeavoured to explore and make sense of the world she lives in.

In the next chapter Hannah's story will be told, highlighting her interests in dynamic back and forth, containing and enveloping schemas.

6

Hannah's Story: Dynamic Back and Forth, Containing and Enveloping Schemas

Background

Hannah was twenty-nine months old when Julie first started to observe her. She attended nursery for two half-day sessions each week. Hannah was the youngest child and only girl in her family. She lived at home with two elder brothers, and her parents. Hannah was brought and collected from nursery by her mum, who was always keen to stay and chat with Hannah's key workers at the start and finish of each session.

From the moment Hannah arrived at nursery each day she had a positive sense of purpose about her. Immediately after hanging up her coat and bag she would set to work on her endeavours for the day, revealing her sense of confidence and her happy, cheerful disposition as she went about her day-to-day business. Hannah seemed to understand that she only had a limited time at nursery; she seemed intent upon making the most of every moment.

Outdoors: 'honey-bee' (24th April; twenty-nine months)

Hannah was already very busy in the outdoor area this morning. She was wearing her nursery coat and wellington boots. Kerry, her key worker, explained how Hannah had put these on all by herself this morning.

Observing Hannah was not an easy task. Trying to not to get in her way, whilst she was continually on the go moving from one activity to the next all around the outdoor area proved to be a difficult task. This morning Hannah's endeavours initially started with her watering the plants, before she proceeded to march around and around the outdoor area many times; sometimes with her arms folded, other times with her arms swinging by her side. She used the scooter to travel back and forth and up and down the outdoor area. At times she did this on one leg, demonstrating her developed sense of balance. The only time I observed Hannah to be stationary was when she was tipping and pouring water onto the ground, all her other exploits demonstrated a huge amount of movement and physicality.

Observing Hannah was at times very demanding and somewhat difficult because she seemed to move swiftly from activity to activity, never seeming to focus on one particular thing. What was most striking was her continual physical activity, her absence of pondering or wondering. Hannah seemed to be constantly on the go moving from one task to another, never seeming to pause, always busy and looking for the next opportunity.

When all of the other children went to get ready for lunch, Hannah began to help her key worker, Kerry, with tidying up the outdoor area. Kerry asked Hannah to collect the balls and place them in the basket. Hannah quickly searched and easily found the balls in many places around the outdoor area. However instead of placing the balls in the basket, Hannah had a different idea! On the far side of the outdoor area was a large piece of guttering attached to the wall, the guttering was fixed at such an angle that allowed objects placed inside to slide down the guttering. Hannah placed a ball at the start of the guttering, I presume she expected to watch the ball roll down the length of the guttering. However, today unexpectedly the ball snagged on a piece of wood that had caught in the guttering (Figure 6.1). The wood had caused a blockage on the guttering making the ball stop half-way down the guttering. This then caused the other following balls to stack up in a row behind. Hannah appeared intrigued, making no attempt to free the caught balls.

One by one Hannah rolled more balls down the guttering, watching intently as each ball moved along the guttering and came to rest. Her concentration appeared intense. Hannah's whole demeanour changed. Suddenly she became captivated and completely engrossed in this activity. Collecting more balls, Hannah continued to add another ball, letting it roll down the guttering, and extending the row of balls as shown in Figure 6.1.

It seemed that Hannah perhaps understood how to make the row longer, and how to extend the shape the balls made. Whilst her focus on the activity only lasted for a short time, Hannah's actions and interest in this activity provided clues into her interest and understanding of the environment.

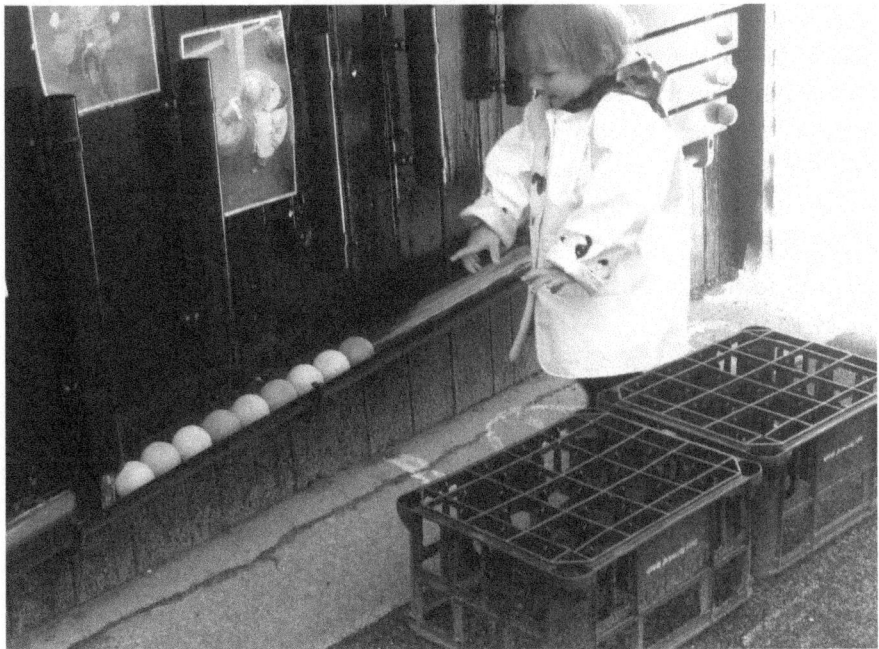

Figure 6.1 A row of balls stuck in the guttering

When she ran out of balls, Hannah seemed to stop and spend a few moments looking and pointing at the balls. It was not possible to hear Hannah's murmurs, but keen not to distract her from her chain of thought, I did not move closer to listen. Kerry, Hannah's key worker, later explained how Hannah regularly liked to line up objects and count them and to sing counting songs using number names up to ten.

Discussion

When considering young children's cognitive development, Nutbrown (2011) describes schemas as being at the 'core' of such development. Suggesting schemas provide the 'fundamental elements ... for the process of learning' (46).

According to Atherton and Nutbrown (2013: 26), looking closely at what children are doing can provide 'insightful views of the subtle, complex details of children's schematic behaviour revealed in their own actions, speech and representations'.

When discussing observation as a research tool, Clough and Nutbrown (2007: 48) introduce the term 'radical looking', suggesting 'this is an exploration, which makes the familiar strange'. Observing young children's activities through a schematic lens provides the opportunity to make the 'familiar strange'. The observer must look for the *form of thought* as well as focusing on the *content* that is being brought in to nourish that *form*. Athey (2007: 66) warns, 'focusing on "content" at the expense of "form" can lead to the conclusion that young children ... are unsystematic or even idiosyncratic'.

Reflecting on the *content* of Hannah's play could suggest that she flits from one activity to another – watering plants, walking around, tipping water, scooting and rolling balls. In contrast, when attempting to make the familiar strange, focusing on Hannah's *actions* could begin to reveal her underlying *forms of thought*. Tipping water and watering plants possibly reveals a vertical trajectory; walking scooting and rolling balls suggests a horizontal trajectory interest. Far from flitting from activity to activity, Nutbrown (2011: 67) identifies that such actions suggest children are 'systematically fitting together relevant experiences'. Meade and Cubey (2008: 38) use the metaphor of a honeybee to describe how children can be observed as they move from activity to activity, collecting experiences to nourish their schemas and starting to make sense of 'abstract characteristics of particular features of their environment'. Atherton and Nutbrown (2013: 50) describe the selection of content to match a form of thought as 'discriminating', suggesting that as young children follow their fascinations they are 'sensitized' to the environment. Through the processes of exploring, thinking and learning, young children are able to pursue and create their own continuities (Atherton and Nutbrown 2013; Nutbrown 2011).

Hannah's fascination with the horizontal was highlighted as she began to tidy up the balls. Placing a ball, one at a time, in the guttering, enabled her to observe the ball as it rolled away from her. It is impossible to know, but perhaps due to the blockage (Figure 6.1), Hannah encountered a new experience. On previous days the balls would have rolled freely and would have possibly bounced off at the end of the guttering, possibly generating an interest in downward movement. The blockage afforded Hannah a new opportunity.

In this moment Hannah is interested in the spatial configuration of the balls as they line up on the guttering, something described by Inhelder and Piaget (1964: 18) as a 'graphic collection'. Atherton and Nutbrown (2013: 49) warn that when children line up objects, the 'dynamic aspect … could easily be missed'. It seems the movement of the balls together with the formation of the arrangement, as well as the adding of another ball to extend the arrangement motivated and fascinated Hannah's curiosity and her form of thought on this occasion. Athey (2007: 114) explains, 'drawings, paintings and models represent both configuration and movement'. This suggests that in this episode the spatial configuration of the balls (Figure 6.1) also represents the sequence of movement required to produce the line of balls for Hannah.

Nutbrown (2011: 68) explains that functional dependency can be understood as the beginning of 'simple cause-and-effect relationships'. Hannah appears to demonstrate an understanding that doing one thing can make something else happen – she seems to have grasped that one action brings about another – for example, pouring the water causes the plants to get wet – therefore the wetness of the plant is functionally dependent upon the pouring of the water. Similarly, in order to increase the row, more balls need to be added, the growing size of the row of balls is functionally dependent upon more balls being added. Hannah's activities can be seen as explorations of functional dependency (Athey 2007) whilst pursuing schemas of vertical and horizontal trajectory.

Athey (2007: 164) purported that language and thought develop independently, but argued the existence of a match between 'forms of thought and appropriate speech'. Using number names to 'count' the balls would demonstrate a match between Hannah's forms of thought and her speech, whilst both her key worker and mother suggest that Hannah can frequently be heard using number names as she counts rows and lines of objects. Unfortunately on this occasion it was not possible to hear Hannah's speech so we can only identify her actions as motor level rather than symbolic.

Athey (2007: 164) suggested that whilst language and thought often develop independently, the existence of a match between 'forms of thought and appropriate speech' gives a strong clue as to the schemas that children are pursuing. It was not possible to hear what Hannah said, to hear if she used number names to correspond with the line of balls; to 'count' the number of balls, but if she used number names to 'count' the balls this would have demonstrated a match between her forms of thought and her speech. Interestingly both Hannah's key worker and mother intimate she is frequently heard using number names as she counts rows and lines of stationary objects.

Observation point:

When you watch the young children playing, consider their physicality. As you observe them, do you become aware of any links between experiences and possible 'forms of thought'?

Recognizing links between *forms of thought* and language development provides practitioners with stronger 'clues' to what children might need next in terms of resources and experiences.

Indoors, Outdoors: 'spatial orientation' (12th May; thirty months)

Water proof jackets and wellington boots are provided for all the children to wear whilst at nursery. From a young age all the children in the nursery are encouraged and supported to develop their own independence in putting on outdoor clothing when it is needed. Wellington boots are stored at floor level in an open fronted cupboard. After selecting a pair of wellington boots the children are encouraged to place their own shoes on the shelf, so ensuring they do not get lost or mixed up.

This morning I observed Hannah confidently and independently put on her wellington boots, then without any prompting placed her shoes on the storage shelf. Once she had successfully selected and put on a raincoat she made her way to the outdoor area.

Outside Hannah selected the large toy car, she climbed inside, shut the door and set of on her journey around the outdoor space. She appeared to be very skilful in the way she drove the play-car around the outdoor area. I noticed that she could make the car go very fast, and Hannah also seemed aware and took care not to bump into the younger children who were also playing outdoors. After several trips around the outdoor area in the car, her focus turned to the water area.

Parking the car she moved to the water area. Spending her time pouring and tipping water from a watering can into a large bowl, the concentration and perseverance displayed within the repetitive actions of the water play identified that Hannah found an aspect of the water play very intriguing this morning. Hannah quickly realized if the water came out through the spout it made a different shape, than when she tipped the watering can further to enable the water to exit through the filling hole at the top as shown in Figure 6.2.

Figure 6.2 The water comes out of the top of the watering can as well as the spout

Could Hannah's interest be in the patterns and shapes the water made as it falls from the watering can? Or was she mostly focused on the effects of her tipping action more generally? When the water came out through the nozzle it made a spraying pattern. When the watering can was tipped further, the water came out in one large stream from the hole in the top, making a different shape and pattern.

It was not long before Hannah's interest in the water moved on. Finding a large metal bowl Hannah strategically placed a couple of small toy figures in the bowl and then proceeded to cover the figures with water. Systematically Hannah ladled water from the large yellow container, until the objects in the bowl were immersed and covered by the water. Hannah appeared unconcerned when other children joined in and added more objects to the bowl. It seemed however that once Hannah was satisfied that the figures were completely immersed and covered in water she lost interest in this activity, and so she moved on with her daily endeavours.

Returning to her journeying Hannah this time selected a bike, she travelled confidently manoeuvring her way backwards and forwards over the narrow wooden bridge in the centre of the outdoor area. Hannah's skill on the bike made this look like an easy task to complete, however I had previously seen several other similar aged children require adult assistance to cross the bridge with the bike.

After several trips back and forth across the bridge, Hannah cycled to the sand pit. Leaning over the side of the bike she quickly filled a plant pot with sand, before continuing her journey around the perimeter of the outdoor area on the bike. Hannah seemed very active, always on the move, and at times it was difficult to follow her play, to recognize her interests, to understand her fascinations, making it difficult to come to know her.

It was not long before Hannah returned indoors. After changing from the wellingtons to her own shoes, she spotted the table in the play area of the room with a large builders tray of rice and a selection of cups, bowls and plates.

Using small cups and bowls Hannah began to scoop the rice, to tip, fill, empty, and contain it within the variety of available containers. Her involvement in the activity persisted over several moments, I moved along side her, I also began filling and emptying the containers with rice. Hannah did not speak, but from time to time glanced up to observe what I was doing. She appeared to be comfortable in accepting me alongside her in the play. Hannah began to sing and hum (unfortunately it was not possible to make out the words or the tune). Hannah arranged the containers; it took a few alterations before she seemed happy with the arrangement, placing the containers in a row. Once she seemed content with her organization she spoke explaining.

Hannah – Three, I count one, two, three.

Julie – Yes you have three, three containers full of rice.

Hannah – I go, I finish, you come.

Julie – Yes I can come, where are we going.

Hannah – Slide, I go on slide.

Hannah quickly moved across the room to the wooden slide. Following her to the slide I counted out loud as Hannah repeatedly came down the slide. I counted ten trips down the slide. After the tenth trip Hannah came and stood with me and together we counted to ten.

The interconnectedness and the continual flow of activities make it difficult at times to follow Hannah. Yet her repeated endeavours, her back and forth movements, her filling and emptying, suggest possible patterns of containing and trajectory schemas.

Discussion

In 'systematically fitting together relevant experiences' (Nutbrown 2011: 67), Hannah productively merges behaviour related to a number of schemas into a continuous flow of exploration and investigation.

- The horizontal back and forth of the car.
- The dynamic vertical interest in the water.
- The containing and envelopment of water and objects.
- The horizontal back and forth with the bike.
- Containing sand, whilst continuing to experience the back and forth movement of the bike.

Such motor actions and perceptual feedback form the foundations for cognitive development and future learning (Atherton and Nutbrown 2013; Athey 2007; Nutbrown 2011). And highlight the importance of both recognizing and understanding 'the subtle ... complex details' such observations convey (Atherton and Nutbrown 2013: 26).

Hannah's use of the bike and car to push herself along suggest a form of thought relating to a horizontal dynamic back and forth schema. Athey (2007: 122) identified that 'when the youngest project children toddled they simply *displaced* themselves. Later they picked up objects and *displaced* those'. On this occasion, Hannah seemed not to displace objects, but used the bike and car to *displace* herself. It is not possible to establish from this observation if she is also exploring 'starting-points' and 'points of arrival', as she *displaces* herself within the outdoor area (Athey 2007: 123). Robson (2012) uses the term 'spatial orientation', suggesting that this is about coming to know environments through a cognitive mapping of a process. 'Developing spatial orientation competencies is a long process' (2012: 172). Walking, scooting and biking around the outdoor environment provides Hannah with the opportunity to take greater perceptual notice. It provides opportunities to gain an understanding of the concepts of length, speed and time as she travels within the spatial environment and sees things from a range of perspectives.

The tipping and pouring of water suggest a dynamic vertical schema. Hannah's exploration of the water is not aimless, she seems to have a clear purpose. Forman (1994) identifies how the properties of different media can 'influence thought' and encourage a 'biased perspective'. Hannah demonstrates purpose by using the dynamic properties of the water to pursue her schema thereby nourishing her schema with interesting content. Initially starting with a red and yellow watering can, she seems to explore and observes the water spray as it flows through the nozzle. She then repeats this with a blue and yellow watering can. Was she testing out the affordances of each of the watering cans? Hannah demonstrates her understanding that to make the water flow through the nozzle is dependent on the angle the watering can is held and tipped and this we suggest fits with Athey's (2007) categorization of similar actions at a functional dependency level.

Athey (2007) suggested that containing and enveloping schemas assist in developing knowledge of insideness, going through and size. This is further supported by Atherton and Nutbrown's (2013: 116) recent research, in which she proposes, 'as children put things inside containers the idea of going through ... is being developed'. Nutbrown (2011: 30) points out that the 'combination and connections of schemas develop into higher-order concepts'. The coordination and connection of Hannah's dynamic vertical trajectory schema and containing and enveloping schema could result in Hannah developing an understanding that by changing how the watering can is tipped (the angle at which it is held), the configuration of the water would be changed as it flows out of the watering can. Forman (1994: 38) states, 'a transformation in the medium that a child can easily produce is an affordance. Each affordance provides the child with a method to explore an idea by transforming the medium'. This suggests that Hannah has understood the affordance of the water and is able to transform its configuration, thus her visual perception of the flow of water changes.

The seemingly unconnected action of putting an object into a bowl and covering it with water could be viewed by Forman (1994) as a further exploration of the properties of water, its ability to be displaced (transported), contained and used to envelope other objects.

Atherton and Nutbrown (2013), Nutbrown (2011), Meade and Cubey (2008) and Athey (2007) all agree that children's schematic explorations can lead to mathematical learning. Atherton and Nutbrown (2013) introduce a scheme of 'Concept – Actions – Possible Learning' to help identify and illustrate children's possible thinking. Adopting this scheme Table 6.1 shows the mathematical learning that Hannah could have experienced as she explored her containing and enveloping schema with the water.

Conversations with Hannah's key worker provided further evidence of her containing and enveloping forms of thought in the following comments about Hannah's preferences and actions in nursery:

> Yes she wraps babies [dolls] up in the bed and the cot, like they are going to bed.
>
> She loves shaving foam. She would rub it right up her arms. When we did body painting she would cover her whole body all her legs as much as she could cover.
>
> When painting, she will cover the whole page
>
> She enjoyed making dens, she just loved being in them.

Hannah continues to match content to her forms of thought as she moves to explore the rice and containers in the indoor environment. The point of particular interest within this observation is her use of numbers. Penderi and Petrogiannis (2011) suggest that culture has a mediating effect on children's development through the orchestrated roles parents play in children's experiences. Super and Harkness (2002) identify that micro environments, such as the child's home, are closely constructed to reflect parental ethnotheories; meaning that parents' cultural behaviours and beliefs are mediated through their parenting practices. Hannah's mother noted:

> She [Hannah] always sits with me and Ryan [older brother], she has her own book, we count and colour, it encourages Ryan to do his work... When we are at the supermarket we count everything, the tins, the crisps, then again when we put it away.

Table 6.1 Hannah's possible mathematical learning

Concept	Actions	Possible learning
Size	Placing objects in bowl	The object fits inside the bowl. The object is small in comparison to the bowl
Volume/capacity	Ladling water into bowl	Full ladle of water only covers a small area of silver bowl
Quantity	Continuing to ladle water into bowl	How many more ladles of water to cover the object

Hannah's number knowledge could be a result of cultural transmission from the everyday activities she is involved in with her family. Through experiences with adults and older siblings who use numbers with her, Hannah has been introduced to naming and counting and encouraged to do so. This supports Munn's (1987) belief that knowledge and use of number names follows a Vygotskian development pattern:

> First, counting appears on the social plane, between people, with children's activity supported by language and goals. After considerable experience of this children internalize the cultural practice of counting. It then appears on the psychological plane, at which point children are able to direct their counting according to adult principles. (Munn 1997: 18)

In contrast, Athey (2007) identifies that the speech children use often reflects their forms of thought (schema) or the content (curriculum). This suggests that the process of cultural transmission is not singularly or totally responsible for learning. Hannah's horizontal trajectory interest is a *form of thought* that provides a meaningful context for the acquisition of abstract number concepts. As her keyworker noted:

> She [Hannah] knows all the number songs, we are always singing them together, we borrow the preschool song box with songs to number ten .... We sing more songs now, Hannah loves numbers. She is always counting things.

Athey (2007) would perhaps compare the process of cultural transmission to that of 'flesh[ing] out' Hannah's cognitive advances (Athey 2007: 167). Of course, there is also a sense here that if the family promotes counting and number use with Hannah – because they think this is what she should be learning – this could inhibit Hannah's further exploration of other concepts. Only close observation with language that matches a child's actions will indicate what children are paying attention to and how their schematic learning might be further nourished.

Observation point:

When watching children who are involved in play activities, consider how schemas might lead to opportunities for young children to develop their mathematical and scientific understanding. How can schemas be supported with exciting and innovative curriculum content which further extends their learning?

Heuristic play: 'stacking' (30th May; thirty months)

Heuristic Play:

Initially developed by Elinor Goldschmied, heuristic play is a particular planned and organized activity offered to the children across the nursery day. Described by Goldschmied and Jackson:

Put simply, it consists of offering a group of children, for a defined period of time in a controlled environment, a large number of different objects and receptacles with which they can play freely without adult intervention. (2004: 128)

Hannah was sitting alone with the heuristic play resources. As soon as she noticed me she smiled at me; I took this as my cue to become involved. I sat down on the mat opposite Hannah. Today Hannah did not appear to be in any rush, in contrast to my observation of 24th April. She was taking her time to rummage and select a range of heuristic play resources. Hannah's selection included Perspex cubes, a wicker ball and several metal tubs and containers, some with lids some without.

Once selected, Hannah began to explore the objects; initially she placed the smaller objects inside the larger objects (see Figure 6.3), before taking them out and repeating the whole process again and again. Hannah spent an extended amount of time (over forty minutes), repeatedly putting objects inside other containers, then taking them out again.

Today was the first time I observed such calm and stillness within Hannah's actions; she appeared to ponder and consider the results of her actions. Her investigative process appeared calm, methodical and organized. Hannah appeared to study how the objects looked when placed inside other objects and containers. As I watched, it seemed to me that she was exploring the visual properties with different objects. At times, depending on the materials Hannah chose, some of the objects would remain visible through the larger object, whilst at other times the objects seemed to disappear inside the larger object. As Hannah continued to explore, she also saw that not all the objects fitted inside each other as shown in Figure 6.3.

Hannah spent time exploring the different metal, plastic, natural and cardboard objects. Putting them inside, taking them out, then retesting. Whilst I cannot presume to know Hannah's thoughts, it seemed to me that she noticed, identified and made new discoveries through her practical engagement with her self-selected

Figure 6.3 Fitting inside and not fitting inside

range of objects. I observed Hannah for over twenty minutes. The room was busy and noisy, but Hannah did not seem to see or hear this today, she remained focused on the one activity and seemed unperturbed by potential distractions.

Discussion

From a vast array of objects Hannah selected seven objects, before finding a space to sit to conduct her exploration and investigation. Neisser (1976: 80) describes this as a perceivers filtering system: 'perceivers pick up only what they have schema(ta) for, and willy–nilly ignore the rest'. Carr (2001: 9) describes knowledge and skills used with a particular purpose in mind as 'situated learning strategies'. Hannah's containing and enveloping schema not only seems to sensitize her to match *content* with her *form of thought*, but also provides the purpose and motivation to learn (Atherton and Nutbrown 2013).

An increasing body of research (Carr 2001; Carr and Lee 2012; Claxton 2008; Dweck 1999; Moss 2010) supports the suggestion that cognitive intelligence is not about mastering new techniques and skills, it is more to do with attitudes, beliefs, emotional tolerance and values. Claxton (2008: 1) defines these as 'dispositions'. Carr (2001: 21) suggests that a useful way of understanding dispositions is seeing children as being 'ready, willing and able ... a combination of inclination, sensitivity to occasion and the relevant skill and knowledge'. Claxton and Carr (2004) consider dispositions to be dynamic, meaning that they are not acquired in a one-off process, but will display themselves in different ways at different times. On this occasion, Hannah's persistence with her containing and exploration is easily spotted, as she remains focused for a twenty-minute period. From a dispositional perspective such persistence can also be identified on other days as Hannah continually returns to repeat and retry activities. Katz (1988: 30) suggests that dispositions can 'be thought of as habits of mind, tendencies to respond to situations in certain ways', a definition that resonates with the form of intrinsic motivation that schema appears to afford young children.

Within the English EYFS (DfE 2014), engagement is identified as an important role in young children's learning (Early Education 2012). Laevers (1976) initially identified the importance of links between children's involvement and learning. Laevers (2000) suggests that high levels of involvement are supported, when children are given choices: 'the more children can choose their own activities, the higher will be their level of involvement' (Laevers 2000: 26).

Hannah's interest, motivation, persistence and involvement continue to be illustrated through her schematic interest. At just thirty months of age, she is already an actor in her own learning.

Observation point:

When you watch the children involved in play, consider how frequently children display deep levels of interest and involvement in their activities. Is it possible to recognize periods of deep and persistent exploration with a particular focus? Consider the environment, how open ended are the materials? Do the resources on offer allow children to explore on different levels? Can they be selected and adapted for multiple explorations and discoveries?

At home: 'shapes and spaces' (21st June; thirty-one months)

I visited Hannah at her home today. When I arrived she was busy, sitting on the living room floor completing a jigsaw puzzle. Hannah continued to focus on the jigsaw puzzle whilst her mum chatted to me, explaining how Hannah enjoyed doing jigsaws and could even do her elder brothers' 'Cars' jigsaw puzzle on her own, without needing the picture. When Hannah successfully completed the jigsaw puzzle she quickly and happily put all the pieces back inside the box.

Hannah turned to face me, seeming pleased to see me. She looked around the room to find and show me many of her toys. It felt that she was happy for me to be in her house, she was giving me her consent.

Hannah wanted her truck. Initially she could not locate it, it took her a little time, she looked in many places. Through her persistence she found the truck and the truck driver. Hannah wanted to put the driver inside the cab on the truck. This was a physically difficult task, as both the cab and truck driver were small and fiddly to manipulate into position. It took several attempts before Hannah was satisfied and the truck was ready. Hannah's insistence to have the driver inside the truck provided further evidence of her containing schema.

Interestingly whilst there was a large empty space on the carpet, Hannah chose to use the TV table as a surface for the truck to move back and forth along; perhaps recognizing the smooth surface, rather than the carpet, would be more conducive to helping the truck roll. She successfully pushed the truck forwards before using the connected cord to pull the truck back. Hannah appeared to know just how hard N to push the truck to make it roll the full length of the TV table, before exerting the correct force to pull it back. She skilfully repeated the action many times.

The back and forth horizontal movement of the truck brought to mind a similarity with Hannah's bodily exploits on the 24th April, in the outdoor area. On that occasion it was Hannah herself who experienced the horizontal back and forth movement as she marched and scooted back and forth around the outdoor area at the nursery. Also Hannah's endeavours on 15th May meant that she had spent time traveling back and forth on the bike, as she repeatedly rode over the bridge. Reflecting back over Hannah's exploits generates a confidence that I was gaining a clearer understanding of her schematic preferences, I was beginning to know and understand her more.

During my visit to Hannah's home her mum made us all a drink. Once finished, the empty cups attracted Hannah's interested. Figure 6.4 illustrates Hannah's discoveries; displaying great care Hannah explored how to fit and stack the cups together. Her small princess cup fitted easily inside the big green mug. As Hannah explored, her mother supported and narrated the investigation.

Mother: Hannah take care, these are real cups

Hannah: My cup, my cup in. My cup in mum's

Mother: Yes it fits inside my cup …

Hannah's explorations with the cups continued for several more minutes, as she repeatedly attempted to stack the cups inside each other.

Hannah: Not fit in, not in my cup. I put away now

Mother: My cup is too big, it will not fit inside… Oh, oh ok put them into the kitchen

Hannah: In sink, I put in sink.

Figure 6.4 New discoveries

Fitting and containing the cups today in her home environment provided a parallel experience to Hannah's explorations with the heuristic play on the 30th May in nursery.

Hannah's interests also appear to include and extend to tidying up – putting objects away – the jigsaws in the box, and the cups in the sink. Whilst the content varies, all of these activities relate to a form of thought consistent with a containing schema. Causing me to wonder is it the size of objects, or the insideness or the static patterns that objects make, which drives her interest – her form of thought?

Discussion

Hannah continues to explore her forms of thinking related to containing and enveloping, freely selecting and matching content from the toys available to her.

Piecing together a jigsaw puzzle enables her to create shapes and spaces that can be used to contain other pieces – but jigsaws provide for only one way of fitting together – flexible resources would have given Hannah the opportunity to explore multiple ways of fitting (as she did with the Heuristic play resources in nursery and the cups at home). Hannah understands that completing the picture (jigsaw) is dependent on her fitting together all of the pieces in a particular fixed order. Hannah's mother explains that 'she loves jigsaw puzzles, she can do most of her brother Ryan's jigsaws, some she can even do without the picture. She puts together the edges then fills in the space in the middle'. This is a task that requires high-level concepts recognizing and understanding of shape and space (Athey 2007).

Completing the jigsaw puzzle involves Hannah in trying to fit and contain two-dimensional shaped pieces. Furthering her understanding of mathematical concepts of width, length, trajectory and orientation, however, the fixed Euclidian space of a jigsaw is limiting in her explorations of such concepts. Hannah is using her developing mathematical knowledge to complete the jigsaw puzzles but she also sees that when the jigsaw goes into the box, the pieces can be contained in other configurations – such topological uses of space offer greater potential for exploration of width, length, trajectory and orientation because they can be manipulated into different orders (as were the heuristic play materials). Hannah did not speak when she was finishing, so it is not possible to know what her thoughts were; however, somewhere in the process it is likely that her thought processes involved an awareness that 'if I turn this around, the straight edge will fit there' indicating 'a busyness of thought upon which increasing complex concepts could be built' (Atherton and Nutbrown 2013: 43).

Hannah's choice of surfaces to push and pull the toy truck along suggests a functional dependency level of thought (Athey 2007). Recognizing particular surfaces can inhibit or support the movement of the truck. Although her thoughts were not accompanied by language, her involvement, and meticulous care in the activity suggest her thoughts could have been – 'must take care, only need a gentle push, a big push will send it too far, it will fall off the end and crash onto the floor' – implying the recognition of a relationship between the amount of force and the distance the truck will travel.

Through an enclosing exploration, Hannah continues to test out her mathematical skills around concepts of size and shape, as she initially places the small cup *inside* the large cup, and then balances the large cup on top of the small cup, before replacing the small cup *inside* the large cup and placing them both *into* the sink. We know from her language that she is focusing on 'inside' (enclosure) and not on 'on top of'. She is using speech to support her actions: 'my cup, my cup in. My cup in mum's... not fit in, not in my cup'. This is further reinforced by her mother's appropriate and elaborating commentary '*Yes it fits inside my cup... My cup is too big, it will not fit inside*'. Matching language with Hannah's actions provides Hannah a 'synchrony with acquired meaning' (Athey 2007: 167), a match between language and her forms of thought. Hannah has already demonstrated her sensitivity to elements in the environment that nourish her schemas and such sensitivity will also include language (Atherton and Nutbrown 2013; Athey 2007; Nutbrown 2011). Athey (2007: 167) highlights that children's speech sometimes 'reflected prominent schemas as well as the content assimilated to schemas'.

Nutbrown (2011: 29) also suggests schemas can provide parents and professionals with a way to become 'in tune with children's cognitive concerns'. A view reflected by Hannah's mother's comments:

> I wouldn't have let her do that (stack the cups) before this (involvement in project). Now I understand better, I realize why she wants to put her truck on the TV cupboard. I find it really interesting, I have really started to watch her, I try to use my speech to support her ideas more.

Such 'tuning in' will help to ensure that Hannah's present encounters feed her future endeavours and the extended knowledge of schematic theory that her mother has acquired puts her in a better position to support Hannah and to understand some of the things she does.

Observation point:

Thinking about your own setting, consider what else might be done to help parents to recognize the learning opportunities available in what appear to be simple play activities. How can knowledge about schematic development be shared with parents in ways that enable them to further support their children's learning at home and in their communities?

Dolls: 'baby play' (27th June; thirty months)

Hannah was already busy in the outdoor area pushing a pram with a 'baby' (doll) inside. She seemed pleased to see me today, greeting me with a huge smile. Within nursery Hannah regularly sees the babies each day when they come into the outdoor area. It seems today Hannah's play includes babies. As I watch her I realize she has a purpose, she takes care to push the pram around the whole of the outdoor area, skilfully manoeuvring and navigating her way around the other objects and toys.

Figure 6.5 illustrates the concentration on Hannah's face as she continued to push the pram and the baby backwards and forwards around the outdoor area. She

Figure 6.5 Taking care with the pram

steered carefully over the bridge and around the objects, taking care not to bump into the younger children who were also playing outdoors. Hannah was mainly able to manage this task alone, however on the occasion she encountered a problem, this is illustrated in Figure 6.5 as a watering can got trapped under the wheel of the pram. When this happened Hannah initiated help from a nearby adult through shouting:

Hannah: I stuck, I stuck

Practitioner: Pull the pram back. I will move the watering can.

Hannah: Pram back, I pull pram.

Practitioner: What are you doing Hannah?

Hannah: Push pram, push baby.

After an extended period of time Hannah's baby play progressed from simply pushing the doll around in the pram. Hannah stopped at the crib, she carefully removed the doll from the pram, expertly she placed the doll at the top of the crib and began to gently rock the crib backwards and forwards. When George came across, Hannah looked at him and spoke.

Hannah: shshsh (as she rocked the crib)

Hannah continued to rock the crib for a few more moments staying close to the crib until George moved away.

Hannah: baby sleep, baby sleep now

Leaving the baby to sleep in the crib she searched around the outdoor area until she found another doll. With what seemed like less care Hannah placed the second baby doll in the yellow water tub. Selecting a small plastic jug she began to tip water over it.

At times this morning it seemed Hannah seemed to treat the doll like a real baby, then at other times it appeared to be used just as an object for her to explore and investigate with.

Later in the morning Hannah was observed helping with the real babies in the nursery. Kerry, her key worker, explained that Hannah liked regularly to spend time helping and playing with the babies when they visit the nursery room. On this occasion Hannah was able to finish her morning in nursery helping the nursery staff to take care of the real babies in the nursery.

Discussion

Hannah confidently recognizes and selects content that continues to nourish her schematic interests. Nutbrown (2011: 40) explains that it is through a consistency of curriculum and pedagogy that young children can become 'active and independent learners'. Athey (2007: 115) suggested that the actions of pushing prams, rocking cribs back and forth, pouring water and placing dolls inside prams, cribs and containers provides evidence of 'action schemas', distinguishing them as a dynamic back and forth, and as a containing and enveloping schema.

Whilst pushing the pram, Hannah is heard to shout, 'I stuck, I stuck'.

Atherton and Nutbrown (2013: 50) describe a similar episode in Henry's play: 'Henry held up his train and tractor before naming them and asserted "I go orry, I go ca"'. Atherton and Nutbrown considered that in holding up the toy and using 'I', Henry was attempting to communicate with the adult, using his language as a social tool. By the same token, when Hannah shouted, 'I stuck, I stuck', she was also trying to gain the attention of the adult, using language to convey a message. At thirty-one months, Hannah's own spoken language is such that she can convey a simple message using utterances of a few words, her accompanying thoughts however, may have been more complex: 'I need help to pull the watering can away from the wheels of the pram.' Hannah understood that in order to attract help, she needed to ask for it. This suggests an understanding of cause and effect between the use of language and gaining adult attention and help. This provides evidence of Hannah's increasing cognitive competencies and of the social nature of learning.

Placing the doll in the crib, and rocking it backwards and forwards, could in its simplest terms be construed as a motor level activity. However, Hannah's use of speech 'shshsh' as she rocks the crib back and forth portrays her intent for George (child) to be quiet, therefore inferring that the baby (doll) needs quiet environment, if it is going to sleep. This suggests Athey's (2007) definition of functional dependency that getting to sleep is often dependent on a quiet environment. Under further consideration, Hannah's use of unsupported speech could also indicate that she is able to view the situation from the babies' perspective, suggesting, as Piaget and Inhelder (1969) identify, that Hannah has the ability to understand events that are happening outside of her self. If this is the case, it suggests that Hannah is able to orientate her thoughts in order to recognize that a baby needs a quiet environment to fall asleep in. On this basis we can suggest that this is a symbolic representational level activity (Athey 2007), evidencing Hannah's continuing developing cognitive advances.

Hannah's following actions of placing a doll in a bowl of water and tipping water over it could be easily construed as undesirable behaviour – she did not appear to be bathing the baby – but merely using the doll as an object to pour water on. The pouring of the water appeared to be the primary activity – the doll was secondary to the experience and it felt that Hannah could have chosen any object to pour water on. In this situation it did not appear that Hannah considered the doll to be a 'baby'. Athey's (2007: 140) perspective on actions that adults find undesirable provides a helpful perspective. She notes that 'two satisfactory aspects of schematic interpretations is that they embrace a wide range of behaviours, and interpretations are positive'. A positive interpretation would suggest that Hannah appears to have reverted to a motor level activity of containing and enveloping, placing the doll in a large container and enveloping it in water using her dynamic vertical trajectory schema. It is not possible to know Hannah's thoughts. She may have initially considered bathing the baby. It is important to understand that Hannah is not displaying any malice towards the doll. She is not trying to drown it, she is, we suggest, continuing to explore her schematic concerns.

Atherton and Nutbrown (2013: 26) reminds us that looking closely at what children are doing can provide 'insightful views of the subtle, complex details of children's schematic behaviour'. This could suggest that Hannah is interested in both the configurative and the dynamic pattern of the water as it flows over the solid body of the doll.

When interacting with the real babies in the nursery, Hannah was, as Rogoff (1990) might suggest, actively putting herself in the role of apprentice, placing herself in a position where she can learn from a more knowledgeable other – in this instance a staff member. Whilst Hannah interacts with the babies, a knowledgeable staff member will be close by using meaningful speech to further link with Hannah's actions and by offering guidance with the babies' safekeeping. This is an example of an adult and child working within the child's zone of proximal development where the more knowledgeable shares and supports the learner (Vygotsky 1978).

Observation point:

When watching children at play it is useful to try to recognize when young children's self-chosen activities provide evidence of their real-world experiences. As you watch young children and work alongside them, consider the ways in which they are starting to recognize the needs of others.

Thinking about using toys and materials in unconventional ways, how do you decide what is acceptable and what is unacceptable? Does an understanding of schematic intent help you to interact and further extend young children's explorations?

Moving objects: 'distances' (14th July; thirty-one months)

Hannah was already busy in the soft play area when I arrived, she responded quickly to my hello, and carried on playing. She seemed to be attempting to move the large soft play shapes around the floor area, some of the largest shapes were as big as Hannah, it was not an easy task she had taken on this morning.

Hannah pushed and pulled the shapes backwards and forwards. She displayed a real determination and persistence with her endeavours. At times it required her whole bodily force to manoeuver the larger shapes around the space. Whilst she was obviously aware of my closeness, she never asked for my help. After an extended time of physical activity Hannah stopped, seeming to take a pause, appearing to muse over her efforts. It was then that I realized she had completely rearranged the shapes to form a horizontal line of shapes along the mirror wall. It had taken Hannah over fifteen minutes to complete this task, yet once done, she happily walked away and left the shapes without so much as a backwards glance.

Hannah independently put on her outdoor clothing and moved into the outdoor area. Initially she chose to sit inside the toy car. She used her feet to move the car. Hannah was competent in moving the car, and could skilfully control and direct it forwards and backwards. After a time Hannah left the car, she began to run and chase around the outdoor space, hiding behind plants, and moving up and down over the bridge. Hannah seemed very energetic this morning, I continued to observe as she spent over ten minutes marching back and forth across the bridge

Returning indoors, her focus once again seemed to alter. Set up on the table was a set of wooden bricks, small wooden figures and wooden cars, two other children were also playing here. Hannah picked up a wooden car, looked at me and made a car noise.

Hannah: Brumbrum ... car go fast.

Hannah pushed the car across table

Hannah: Car go ... crash ... I make car go far ... I make big crash.

Figure 6.6 captures the moment Hannah pushed the car making it bump and knock down a small pile of wooden bricks that had been previously built and left at the edge of the table. Hannah quickly rebuilt the pile of bricks and repeatedly pushed the car making it role into the bricks. Each time the car hit the bricks Hannah said 'crash'. Hannah used more bricks to build a higher pile. Smiling at me Hannah said: 'I make a big crash'. Hannah's face told me she had enjoyed this activity, at times her excitement had made her jump up and down, and laugh when the car hit and knocked down the bricks to make a big crash.

Figure 6.6 Making the car crash

Hannah obviously understood how to make the car crash, and how to make a big crash, a task she had found very satisfying. Humour is an indicator of a child's understanding of what is happening (Chapman 1977).

Interpreting Hannah's understandings and interests has been a complex task. Whilst the content can be obvious and match with her environments continue to nourish Hannah's schemas – her forms of thinking have required close observation and deep understanding, reflection and a freedom of time – such learning cannot be hurried and a form of patient pedagogy is often called for. I have been privileged to witness the continual interactions and investigations of how Hannah's exploits at home and in the nursery have united to generate greater cognitive competency and this has become more apparent to me over time.

Discussion

Hannah continues to illustrate the actions of the 'honeybee' (Mead and Cubey 2008: 38), spending the morning collecting experiences to feed and nourish her schemas. Her actions display continuity as she selects content to feed her interest in a dynamic horizontal trajectory schema (Atherton and Nutbrown 2013; Athey 2007; Nutbrown 2011). To the untrained eye her playful and physical episode with the soft play could be seen as aimless and pointless. Conversely pushing, pulling, sliding and rolling the large soft play shapes would be seen by Gardner (1984: 211) as providing opportunity to 'judge the timing, force and extent of our movements and to make necessary adjustments in the wake of this information'. This is the stuff of civil engineering, and of physicists. Gardner (1984: 207) identifies the importance of developing 'mastery' of body motion, describing this as 'bodily-kinaesthetic' or 'bodily intelligence' and through this Hannah has achieved a personally set goal which involved the force of her whole body and the perception of shape and movement.

Hannah's persistence and resilience during this activity demonstrates a deep level of involvement, she had to engage in thought processes around: shape, flatness, force, curved shapes, pushing, rolling, bigness, comparative size and weight. Through a process of trial and error Hannah manoeuvred and lined up the shapes one after another. Atherton and Nutbrown (2013: 49) suggests that 'through these trajectory behaviours, an understanding of higher order concepts such as length, distance and addition germinates'. Within the outdoors, Hannah continues this exploration, pushing the car, running and marching around, exploring the motion of back and forth, stopping, starting, speed and gradients. Payne and Isaacs (2008) claim that such activities allow for continuity in the mastering of children's gross bodily motor intelligence, and they warn that a lack of such opportunities and experiences can lead to gaps in children's future learning potential. The physicality of learning is shown clearly in this example – and we know that young children often employ their whole body in their play and explorations and, thus, in their thinking and learning.

Nutbrown (2011: 77) insists that when 'pedagogy matches children's persistent forms of thoughts', a breadth of learning can take place. Gardner (1984: 207) would perhaps argue that Hannah has developed a 'mastery' of fine motor control. She understands and possesses the skills to move equipment and materials in a predetermined way – according to her own plan. At thirty-one months of age, building and stacking the bricks, pushing the car with a measured amount of force to thrust it forwards across the table, but not so it falls off, displays developing mastery in both Hannah's fine motor skills and developing mathematical knowledge. To make a 'big crash', Hannah understands that she needs an increased number of bricks – and perhaps a little more force. Hannah stacks more bricks to make a taller pile. Hannah's use of speech appears not only to accompany her actions, but also to instigate a social interaction (Piaget 1959), sharing her intentions: 'I make car go fast', and thereby conveying meaning to her actions: 'I make car crash'. Hannah demonstrates an understanding of the relationship between the force (pushing the car) and the speed of the car. Athey (2007) would suggest that Hannah's own internalized experience of movement through a horizontal trajectory allows her to know in advance what will happen to the car when she pushes it. Hannah is able to use her knowledge of actions together with speech to provide a commentary of the action before it has occurred. If this is the case Hannah's speech followed by her actions could be categorized at a thought level by Athey (2007). Of course, if Hannah had not mastered the skill of quickly building up the tower of bricks, she would have found the act of repeatedly crashing them down much less satisfying. Children usually find crashing towers of bricks satisfying once building them up is no longer a challenge to them, and so the crash becomes satisfying – and even amusing.

Observation point:

As you watch children involved in play, consider whether sufficient time and effort is given to allow fragments of observations to be pieced together to discover young children's schemas which with reflection can uncover their true potential and complex cognitive understanding of the world.

Consider the moments that children find funny – does this indicate mastery of a skill or a particular piece of knowledge? How does such humour link with children's schemas?

Final thoughts

In this chapter we have illustrated what can at times be a difficult, messy and ambiguous process of recognizing and coming to know an individual child and their schematic interests. Nutbrown (2011: 67) describes Jeanette as a child 'who apparently flitted from one experience to another: house play, drawing, water, sand, clay, making crackers for imaginary party, giving presents, playing at cooking'. Hannah's story is similar, her actions included watering plants, marching around, tipping water on the floor, riding bikes and scooters, stacking containers, lining up balls, crashing cars, pushing prams. From the point of view of the observer, Hannah's wide-ranging actions and endeavours regularly generated a huge amount of information, much of which was initially very confusing and often conflicting and with no obvious 'fit'.

Nutbrown (2011: 67) suggests that far from flitting from activity to activity, children may well be fitting together relevant experiences to match their schematic interest. Hannah and Jeanette both selected 'a set of experiences bound together by an almost invisible thread of thinking'. Athey (2007: 66) warns against 'focusing on content at the expense of form', however it is not always easy to recognize such fine threads, or forms of thought. It is a dynamic, complex and messy process (Hayes 2008: 435) which requires skills and patience.

Recognition of the 'fine thread' of Hannah's schematic intents required observations to be layered and overlapped, allowing Julie to move within and across the evidence collected from week to week, to ponder over the connections in Hannah's sensitized selection of resources. Only through trusting Hannah's own judgments and choices of resources was Julie, over time, able to begin to recognize the fine yet perceptible threads that revealed Hannah's forms of thought. Once recognized, Hannah's previously 'unsystematic' (Athey 2007: 66) actions not only made sense, but also illustrated Hannah to be what Nutbrown (2001: 40) would call an 'active and independent learner', a social actor in her own life and learning.

Hannah's strong sense of her own purpose is further illustrated by her pleasure in and use of number names. Hannah is able to use number names up to ten. This is not a skill first initiated in the nursery or directly taught at home. Athey (2007) and Super and Harkness (2002) would suggest it is through a combination of cultural transmission processes and Hannah's horizontal trajectory interest of her form of thought that provides a meaningful context for the acquisition of abstract number concepts. This in turn causes Hannah's key worker to provide further content to nourish, consolidate and extend her number knowledge, once again suggesting Hannah is a social actor in her own learning.

This chapter has shown that when adults have a deep knowledge of pedagogy, child development and schemas, combined with trust and respect, young children can really thrive and become the centre of their own learning. Hannah's story also shows the need for patient, persistent observation over time in order to understand the forms of thinking in which she was engaging. Such things cannot be hurried.

The next chapter will introduce Emily whose narrative observations will tell of her interest in dynamic back and forth, containing, enveloping and transporting schema.

7

Emily's Trajectory, Containing, Enveloping and Transporting Schemas

Emily was twenty-three months old when Julie began the observations. Emily attended nursery for three half-day sessions each week. She is the only child in her family, living at home with her mother and father.

Emily arrives happily at the start of each nursery session, calmly and quietly saying goodbye to her mother. She usually displayed a spirited and cheerful disposition, with a vivacious sense of fun, and an animated smile. Sometimes, Emily could appear a little reserved, choosing to watch the day-to-day goings-on, before trying and experiencing activities herself. However, once involved, Emily consistently displays high levels of energy and purpose within her daily exploits.

Apprentice: Continuities of thought
(24th April; twenty-three months)

Emily was already in the outdoor area, displaying signs of deep levels of concentration as she walked back and forth across the bridge. Glancing up, she spotted me, smiled and continued with her actions. Emily initially seemed to pay little attention to either me or the other adult staff member who was involved in singing and marching around the outdoor area with several other children.

When Emily spotted her key worker, Leanne, at the water butt her actions changed. She quickly crossed the outdoor space to join in with Leanne and the water play. Swiftly she selected a container and proceeded to fill it with water; once full Emily tipped the water out. Emily's face revealed her interest as she watched the water fall, it almost appeared to form a long straight line as it left the container and flowed to the ground. Figure 7.1 shows Emily's focus and interest as Leanne encourages her to explore the water.

Figure 7.1 Exploring the water

Emily continues to explore the movement of the water for several more minutes with Leanne narrating the sequence of events and actions.

Leanne: Emily is tipping the water… Can you see the water… the water falls down… Can you do it again… Emily make the water fall again.

Emily quickly became absorbed with the activity. When Leanne moved away, Emily seemed undeterred; she continued to fill containers with water and then to empty them. Emily's investigations continued for over fifteen minutes as she used a variety of watering cans and a small blue jug, to aid her exploration of tipping and pouring water.

Emily next spotted Leanne near the musical drum. Joining Leanne, together they played on the big drum. Emily used the shakers as drum sticks, moving them up and down to hit the drum. Whilst Leanne was present, Emily's interest in the drum remained; however, without Leanne's encouragement she quickly lost interest. When she could no longer see Leanne outside Emily moved indoors.

Indoors two young children were trying to climb the steps to the slide and Leanne helped the younger children on the slide. Emily joined in. She patiently waited to take her turn to climb up the steps and then walked down the slope of the slide. Emily joined in with Leanne and the other children, Leanne narrated as the children walked up the steps and down the slide. Needed by another child Leanne moved away from the slide. Emily watched Leanne leave the slide, but she chose to remain at the slide, repeatedly climbing up the steps and walking down the slope. I had been observing Emily using the slide for a few moments before I began to narrate out loud her actions, I moved closer and continued to narrate Emily's actions.

Julie: Emily is on the slide ... Emily can go up and down ... Emily at the top ... Emily at the bottom.

Emily made no verbal response; but she did keep smiling. I took this as a cue to continue. After many trips up and down the slide on her feet, Emily announced, 'I sit'. She then proceeded to slide down the slide on her bottom, repeating this action many more times.

Discussion

Within early years, the importance of young children feeling safe and emotionally secure is becoming increasingly vital and more accepted and understood (Clare 2012; Gerhardt 2004; Page et al. 2013). The Field (2010) report highlights that 'children's life chances are most heavily predicated on their development in the first five years of life' (5). Field (2010) identifies social and emotional development in young children as a contributing factor to a successful adulthood, a view further supported by Allen (2011), who reports that:

> babies are born with 25 per cent of their brains developed, and there is then a rapid period of development so that by the age of 3 their brains are 80 per cent developed.
>
> In that period, neglect, the wrong type of parenting and other adverse experiences can have a profound effect on how children are emotionally 'wired'. This will deeply influence their future responses to events and their ability to empathise with other people.
>
> This is not to say that development stops at age 3 – far from it; but the research indicates that we need to intervene early to make sure that our children get the best possible start in life. We need to keep supporting them throughout childhood in ways, which help them reach the key milestones of social and emotional development. (xiii)

Clare (2012) describes how, within care settings, key person or key worker systems are used to support young children in developing close relationships.

Such relationships allow children to form multiple attachments. Page and Nutbrown (2008: 24) note that 'some may argue that a lack of multiple attachments in the early part of life could also be detrimental to babies' social development'. It would appear that Emily has developed such an attachment and relationship towards her key worker, Leanne. Emily appears to ignore the support from a less familiar adult as she moves back and forth across the bridge, choosing instead to actively seek out her key person. Elfer et al. (2012) describe the key person role as one that:

> Makes sure that, within the day-to-day demands of the setting, each child feels special and individual, cherished and thought about by someone in particular while they are away from home. It is as though the child was camped out in the key person's mind or that there is an elastic thread of attachment that allows for being apart as well as for being together. The child will experience a close relationship that is affectionate and reliable. (23).

Robert's (2010) notion of the role of a companionable apprentice seems helpful here. In this scenario, Leanne has become Emily's key person (Elfer et al. 2012), allowing and supporting Emily to become her apprentice. Emily observes, as Leanne models and demonstrates, before Emily then begins to explore for herself. Atherton and Nutbrown (2013: 158) report that as a key worker, the adult's role involves the identification of the child's intrinsic motivations, implying that Leanne 'should not only respond to, but also anticipate' Emily's interests and motivations. This suggests that Leanne's presence and actions within this observation are not merely coincidental, but rather that Leanne has come to know Emily as a result of careful observation and that Emily has developed an attachment to Leanne. With such obvious emotional security in place, it would seem that Emily is ready to join in the culture of learning. Page (2016: 88) argues that modern attachment theory 'informs and structures practitioners' behaviours with children ... that takes account of the myriad insights that research continually provides (in neuroscience no less than the psycho/socio-cultural theory)'. She further asks what the learning environment in a setting that prioritizes secure, attached relationships should look like. Does a setting that prioritizes attachment look any different from that in a setting where attachment is a part of a whole range of priorities? We suggest that it is Emily's secure relationship with Leanne that gave her the confidence to try actions and experiences again and again, and that Leanne's presence enabled what might also be called sustained, shared thinking (Sylva et al. 2004).

Whilst Emily chose to join Leanne in particular activities, a constant thread can be recognized to be running through her choices, described by Athey (2007: 113) as 'commonalities and continuities ("cognitive constants")'. The up and down movement across the bridge, the tipping of the water, the vertical movement of the shakers and the up and down movements on the slide all suggest 'dynamic vertical schemas' (115). Nutbrown (2011: 46) would consider that at only twenty-three months of age Emily is already demonstrating her ability to create her 'own continuities in the process of exploring, thinking and learning'.

Throughout the observations, there is little evidence of Emily's use of speech. Yet in her use of the words 'I sit', it seemed that Emily was trying to engage Julie's attention. Emily wanted to be heard, she wanted to be listened to. We can characterize this as socialized speech (Piaget 1959: 20) in that it is Emily's attempt to share her thoughts, as she confidently furthers her physical and bodily exploration of a dynamic vertical trajectory.

Observation point:

When watching the children in your setting, consider what practices are, or might be put, in place to ensure that young children are comfortable and confident in their environments? What place does Modern Attachment Theory have in the setting?

What importance is given to allowing children time to make their own choices both of what materials to explore in their play and which adults they wish to relate to?

Containing: 'insideness' (10th May; twenty-three months)

Emily was amongst a group of four children involved in an activity around the water butt. Emily together with the three other children had discovered bubbles in the large yellow water tub. Emily's face illustrated the excitement of this discovery. I approached and asked, 'What have you found?'

'Bubbles, bubbles, bubbles' Emily repeated, whilst continuing to dip her hand in and out of the bubbles.

As Emily enthusiastically thrust her hands into the yellow tub that was full of bubbles, she discovered a toy animal. Lifting it out of the bubbles, Emily spent several moments examining it, turning it around. She did not speak, but seemed to momentarily pause as she examined the toy animal which was covered in bubbles. Rather than replacing it back in the bubbles she walked to the toy car. Emily placed the bubble-covered animal into the small compartment at the back of the car as illustrated in Figure 7.2. It emerged that there was already a toy animal in this compartment. This may have been Emily's previous work.

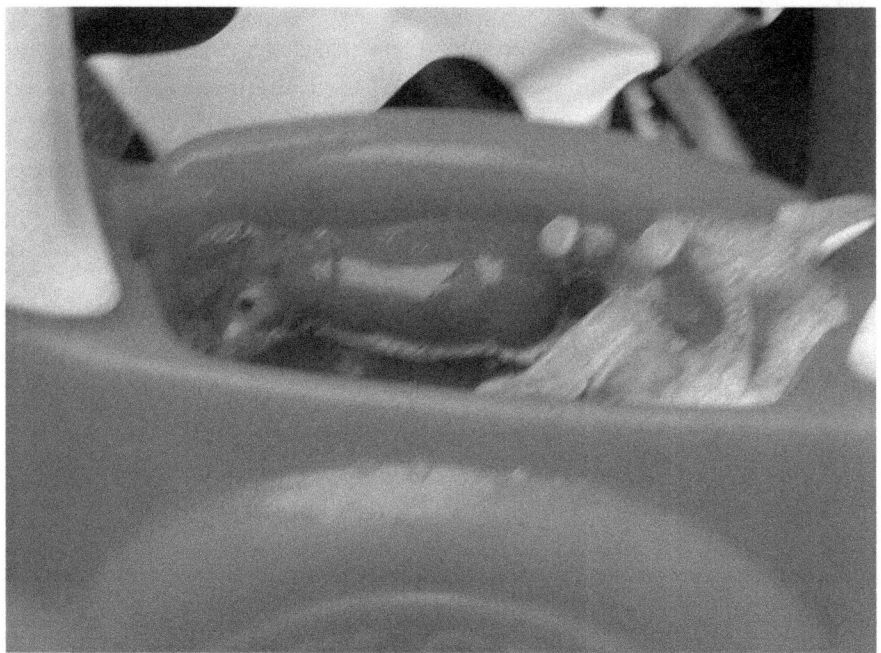

Figure 7.2 Toys placed in the compartments

Emily climbed into the car. She held the steering wheel, closed the door and sat inside the car, seemingly making little attempt to move the car.

Emily remained in the car. She seemed to be sitting and watching the other children as they moved around the outdoor area. When approached by a younger child, Emily held onto the door to prevent it from being opened. Emily appeared quite determined to hold her ground not moving from within the car. The confrontation lasted for a few moments. Neither Emily nor the younger child seemed particularly concerned by the outcome which felt to me to be a situation they have both experienced previously.

Emily remained inside the car, gradually and slowly beginning to use her feet to push the car around the outdoor area. Eventually Emily climbed out of the car. She removed the toys from the rear compartment (Figure 7.1), throwing them to the ground, before placing her hands inside the compartment. Emily placed her whole weight onto the car to push it forwards, whilst keeping her hand inside the compartment. Emily continued to push the car until another child climbed into it. Emily turned and told the child 'I finish, I done'.

Emily returned indoors, gesturing to an adult to help her with her coat. Emily's attention focused on her shoes. Emily's key worker explained how she loves shoes, describing how when Emily first joined the Tweeny room she initially spent her first few morning sessions simply putting on her shoes and Wellington boots and taking them off again. When I visited them at home in May, Emily's mother also confirmed her interest in shoes, describing when on a visit to the shoe shop 'She got these shoes in Clarks, then she was showing everyone around town ... In her pram going "shoes", "shoes" to complete strangers ... She can get frustrated with the buckle ... she is trying to figure it out'. Emily spent several minutes attempting to fasten her shoes before gesturing that she needed some help. Once successfully fastened Emily's attention quickly turned to the indoor water tray.

Emily quickly became very involved, using a selection of jugs to tip and pour the water, she seemed not to notice the other children that came to play alongside her. Finding the water wheel, she cleared a space in the water tray, stood the water wheelupright and began to pour water into the top of the water wheel. Emily closely observed as the water ran down and made the wheels turn. She repeated this many times. Emily seemed very amused by this, as she repeatedly laughed each time the wheels turned. As I observed it became obvious that Emily understood how to make the waterwheel turn. However her face continued to display the surprise and delight each time she successfully caused the wheel to turn.

Emily continued with her purposeful exploits, tipping and pouring water from a variety of different-sized jugs and containers, for over forty minutes during the remainder of the morning.

Discussion

When describing Henry's containing and enveloping behaviour, Atherton and Nutbrown (2013: 36) explain that 'he regularly placed assorted objects (sand, soil, stones, dry pasta, crayons, toy animals, Lego chalks) into a variety of containers and enclosed himself within or underneath a range of items'. Emily's actions suggest similarity in her forms of thought, as she also places objects inside others. Emily's interest in shoes, taking them on and off, could also be considered as part of this schema. This infers that Emily uses both her body and a selection of resources to pursue her containing and enveloping schema. Simply identifying Emily's schemas is not sufficient; if we are to 'extend learning', we must first gain a greater understanding of their thinking and then use this insight to offer new and extending activities (Nutbrown 2011: 18).

When considering Emily's detailed actions, it is difficult to differentiate between containing and enveloping due to both actions being observed simultaneously. Similarly Athey (2007) found it difficult to 'quantify coordinations of schemas', suggesting enveloping and containing schemas can prove 'difficult to differentiate between' (146). Emily contains and envelops her hands in bubbles, before containing and enveloping toy animals in a water-filled hollow section at the back of the car. Emily climbs inside the car, and in closing the door, she contains herself inside – this is one interpretation – as is Emily using the car as an enveloping space? Finally, in placing her hands in the water inside the hollow at the back of the car, Emily could be considered to be both enveloping and containing her hands. When we consider that the same curriculum content can nourish these schemas, we can also see that there is little need to pinpoint precisely which is dominant because when given open-ended materials which children can manipulate to their own ends, it is *they* who determine the content that provides the best fit to their schematic pursuits. As Piaget and Inhelder (1969: 5) explain, experiences are modified by the child and 'become incorporated into the structure'. This resonates with Athey's (2007) understanding that, as children gain experience with such a variety of content, they are able to assimilate and construct further information and meaning within their forms of thought, possibly extending and even constructing new *forms*.

Atherton and Nutbrown (2013: 158) indicate that it is only through careful observation that we 'can come to know and more fully understand, what young children are actually thinking about when they play'. Emily's persistence with her forms of thought through a range of different content could signify an inherent interest in 'insideness' whether that is through 'containing' or 'enveloping' or a combination of the two.

Without the accompaniment of speech, Emily's containing and enveloping activities would be considered as motor level actions. Whilst Athey (2007: 140) explains that such actions are an extension of 'earlier locomotion skills', these actions must also be considered as providing valuable experiences of spatial relationships. Indeed, Athey (2007) and Nutbrown (2011) both consider how ideas of inside, outside and containing can develop into later mathematical knowledge of measure and space.

Athey (1990) states '*functional dependency relationships* manifest when children observe the effect of action on objects or materials' (70). Emily's explorations with the waterwheel indicate an understanding that, in order to turn the wheel, she needs to tip the water, suggesting that she understands that the turning of the wheel is functionally dependent on the water. Athey (1990: 70) explains that the understanding of functional dependencies 'arises from the application of earlier schematic behaviours'. This suggests that Emily's previous dynamic trajectory explorations on the slide and the tipping of water have supported and influenced her developing 'intelligence'. Piaget and Inhelder (1969) write:

> There is a continuous progression from spontaneous movements and reflexes to acquired habits and from the latter to intelligence. The real problem is not to locate the appearance of intelligence but rather to understand the mechanism of this process (5).

Viewing Emily's actions through a schematic lens provides the opportunity to better understand the 'mechanism of this process' (5).

Whilst we are unable to know Emily's thoughts, her reaction and repeated laughter suggests enjoyment. Emily was expecting the wheel to turn before it actually did, implying Emily was able to carry out this operation in her mind before completing the motor action. She seemed able to anticipate the movement. If this is the case, Emily's experiences illuminate and illustrate Piaget's notion that 'thought consists of internalized and coordinated action schemas' (1959: 357). Emily's involvement and ease with this activity is more than a functional dependency understanding between the water and the wheel movement. Emily's laughter suggests that she is able to anticipate what is going to happen, that she had her own theory – developed through previous experience. This supports Athey's (1990: 70) view that functional dependency can be considered 'as a subdivision of thought level'.

Observation point:

Schema? So-what! As you watch the children involved in play you may be able to identify certain actions as indicative of particular schemas. Many practitioners get quite good at 'schema spotting'. But this is only part of the process. Recognition of a schema is not enough!

In order to extend children's thinking and learning it is necessary to look closely at what is it about a child's train of thought that interests and fascinates the child? How can this be further supported and extended? What materials, experiences and language might you offer by way of extension?

Intrinsic motivation: 'play and struggle' (19th May; twenty-three months)

Emily is busy on the indoor wooden slide; repeatedly she climbs up the steps and slides down the slope. I observed for several minutes before she noticed me. Smiling in acknowledgement of my presence Emily continued on the slide, sometimes running down, sometimes walking down and sometimes sliding on her bottom. When other children joined in the activity, Emily happily took turns, seeming to take care not to knock or bump into her friends. Emily's obvious pleasure and excitement is indicated by her huge grin and shouts of laughter, as she descended the slide. Whilst at times, practitioners provided support to ensure the younger children's safety; I tried to keep my distance so as not to interrupt Emily's focus.

In time Emily approached me and smiling, she took my hand and led me to the other side of the room. Here she selected a wooden animal shape jigsaw puzzle. Emily took all the pieces out and then began to replace the animal shapes into the spaces. Each time Emily replaced a shape, she attempted to name the animal saying 'orse, 'abbit, duck, pig, sheep, chick'. Emily quickly completed two puzzles.

It was interesting to notice how, in an instant, Emily's whole demeanour had changed from the loud, lively and full bodily physicality observed on the slide, to that of quiet and calm, as she controlled the small precision movements of matching and containing shapes within the puzzle.

Moving on from the animal puzzle Emily selected a wooden puzzle that contained three-dimensional shapes (cylinder, cube and cuboid) of different sizes. Emily explored the shapes in the new puzzle. Removing some animal shapes from the first puzzle, Emily effortlessly placed the new wooden block shapes into the empty animal spaces. She did not speak whilst completing this task and took her time, seeming to ponder. Emily's interest then moved back to the wooden block puzzle. Taking her time, she attempted to replace the wooden cuboid shape. Whilst Emily seemed to understand which space it should fit into, she found it difficult to align the corners which meant that initially the shape appeared to not fit into the space. Emily was unable to get the shape to fit into the correct space so I offered some verbal encouragement to support her attempts. Emily demonstrated persistence, continuing to wiggle the shape around the space. At first this did not seem to work, however Emily's continual pursuit of this strategy meant after a few more moments the shape slotted in. I expected Emily to be pleased with her success, however this did not seem to be the case!

Seeming to forget my presence, and without a backward glance, Emily left the uncompleted puzzle and walked immediately and directly back to the slide where she stood at the base of the steps for several moments. I wondered, as she stood there, if she was replaying the shape puzzle, questioning why it had not worked as she had expected it to. Within a few minutes, Emily had returned to her lively and fun exploits on the slide.

Discussion

Emily continues to explore her dynamic vertical trajectory schema through the ascent and descent of the slide (Athey 2007). In a similar way to Abby, Emily also uses different bodily movements to possibly gain a deeper perceptual understanding of the descent. For Athey (1990: 70) 'operations that can be carried out in the head' are initiated from 'sensory and perceptual information accompanying motor actions'. So, in the act of ascending and descending the slide, Emily continues to develop her internalized understanding of vertical trajectories. These often precede the making of vertical marks, because it seems that children need to feel the physical movement before they are able to represent it graphically.

Emily's experience on the slide appears to have been positive, the smile she had when finishing seemed to be one of pleasure about her own cognitive development, rather than a reaction to seeing me.

Atherton and Nutbrown (2013: 50) describe children's selection of content as 'discriminating' and 'sensitized', meaning that children match and nourish their schema, their forms of thought, through available environmental resources.

Emily's selection of jigsaw puzzles reveals her containing and enveloping schema.

Using appropriate speech *orse, abbit, duck, pig, sheep, chick to* 'accompany [and] to reinforce' (Piaget 1959: 17) her actions, Emily's playfulness could portray her 'cognitive confidence' when completing the jigsaw (Athey 1990: 50).

Such 'cognitive confidence' appears not to be reflected in Emily's attempt at the shape puzzle. Athey (2007: 51) proposes children's 'functioning ranges from struggle through practice to play'. It is plausible that Emily experiences 'cognitive discomfort' when she 'struggles' to fit the cuboid in the puzzle. Although eventually succeeding, Emily's 'cognitive discomfort' with this experience could be why she left the activity quite quickly.

However, this is another example of the limitations of jigsaws when Euclidian space offers only one solution. If Emily were seeking to fit the shape into a more flexible space – a box or a bag – she would have succeeded because topological space offers more possibilities. Dickson, Brown and Gibson (1993) describe topological properties as 'global properties which are independent of size or shape' (13) and Euclidean properties as 'those relating to size, distance and direction and hence leading to the measurement of lengths, angles, areas and so on' (14). Nutbrown (2011: 89) notes that:

> Children explore space in flexible ways: manipulating shapes into spaces; arranging shapes into regular and irregular patterns; and creating patterns in space as they draw and paint. In the light of such varied manipulation of shape and space, the usefulness of jigsaws that require children to fit shapes together in a single set fashion, and colouring books that offer only the opportunity to fill in fixed spaces of colour, need to be questioned.

Observing Emily's behaviour through a schematic lens provides the opportunity to gain a greater understanding of her cognitive development, from playfulness indicating 'the well established' to the 'struggle' of gaining new knowledge (Athey 2007: 51). At this point it is not possible to gauge if Emily's struggle was due to her mathematical knowledge of shape and space or her kinaesthetic fine motor control. What is certain is that Emily's intrinsic motivation, her forms of thought, will ensure that she continues this development journey. This provides evidence that Emily's schematic behaviour contributes to her becoming a social actor in her own life and learning.

Combining experiences: 'transporting'
(21st May; twenty-four months)

I had arranged to visit Emily at home today, when I arrived Emily was waiting at the front door. She watched as I parked my car outside her house and walked up the garden path. She seemed very pleased to have a visitor.

Inside the sitting room, there was a neat row of toys. Emily's mum explained how 'Granddad teaches her to put things away when she has finished – she loves doing it ... she likes putting things away – I've always been tidy'.

Emily and her mum were sitting on the settee sharing story books. Rather than walking to select a new book, Emily preferred to crawl on all fours across the carpet, using her chin to gently nudge the selected book back across the carpet. After a while, Emily chose to stay on the carpet. Lying on her tummy, to look through the books independently.

After a time Emily's focus turned to her large pink sit on play truck. Before sitting on the truck Emily inspected the telephone handset as shown in Figure 7.3, taking it off and replacing it with ease. The circular parts of the handset clicked into the shaped space. Fitting the circular telephone head, back into the slot on the truck is a similar concept to the experience Emily had with the wooden block shape puzzle at the nursery. Unlike on that occasion, today Emily completed this self-initiated task with ease.

Emily sat on the truck and expertly manoeuvred her way around the furniture in the sitting room, circling the room several times before her attention turned to a small soft football placed on the top of a small neat pile of her toys. Leaving the truck she proceeded to kick and dribble the football around the furniture in the room. The game continued until Emily was distracted by my camera case falling

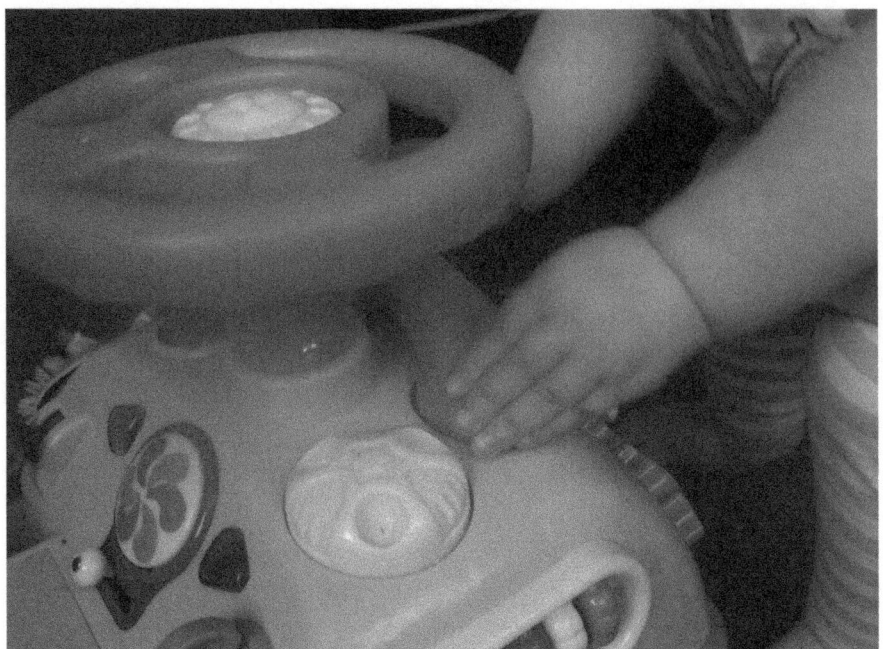

Figure 7.3 Checking the phone

into her path. Emily's mother laughed as she explained: She likes bags, she fills and empties… the stuff she puts in them!

Emily explored the camera case. She peered inside it. The case had a magnetic catch. Emily folded the lid down. As the catch clicked shut she smiled, Emily practiced opening and closing the lid, she did this several times, appearing very thoughtful whilst handling the case gently throughout the whole time.

Once again, Emily quickly moved from a high level of physical activity to a deeply purposeful exploration. Perhaps Emily wished her shoes would fasten with such ease, why could she fasten the camera case, but still struggle with her shoes!

It is possible looking inside the camera case triggered Emily's next flow of thoughts and her actions. Picking up a pile of books, she placed them inside her toy pram. Emily then found her baby doll and placed it inside the pram, with the books. She then pulled over the fitted pram cover so that the contents were now completely contained within the pram and hidden from sight.

Although rather large in size, Emily managed to push the pram and its contents around the living room avoiding the settee several times, before it eventually became wedged between the settee and the chair. When the pram became stuck Emily did not ask for help, but her facial expressions displayed the deep level of concentration that was required as she attempted to free the pram. Using her whole body to push and control the movement of the pram, Emily successfully steered and directed the pram around the settee – demonstrating her developing knowledge and understanding of shape, space and bodily intelligence.

Discussion

Gardner (1984: 18) argued that 'the individual is continually constructing hypotheses and thereby attempting to generate knowledge: he [*sic*] is trying to figure out the nature of material objects in the world'. When Atherton and Nutbrown (2013: 38) described Henry exploring insideness through a range of environmental content, they assert that the 'objects were not of consequence, they were just to hand'. This also seems to be true with regard to Emily's choice of dolls, drinking cups and books. This resonates with Neisser's (1976: 56) description of schema as 'a pattern of action as well as a pattern for action'. Emily's inherent tendencies influence her forms of thought – her pattern of action – they sensitize her to select objects she can contain and envelope – her pattern for action. Emily's interest and inclination to enjoy tidying up is not a coincidence but would be seen by Nutbrown (2011) as a form of nourishment for her containing and enveloping schema.

Atherton and Nutbrown (2013) explain that young children's schema provide a 'blueprint through which higher order conceptual understanding' can be gained. It is anticipated that Emily's initial motor action activities will lead to the development of higher order thinking, meaning that through repeatedly and playfully placing objects of different shapes and forms inside other objects (Athey 2007), Emily will continue to gain both sensory and perceptual feedback, thus enabling her to successfully accommodate and assimilate information into her forms of thought – her schema.

Emily becomes immersed in her investigation, seeming to contemplate and perhaps to wonder 'what can I do with these objects'? Emily discovers that she can contain many objects *inside* the pram. She can also move the pram around with the objects *inside* it. According to Piaget and Inhelder (1969) at twenty-four months, Emily's focus within this inquiry is not object permanence. Emily's seemingly new interest could be the result of 'newly established connections integrated into an existing schematism' (Piaget and Inhelder 1969: 5), the construction of a new transporting schema. Transporting objects in the pram requires a level of bodily kinaesthetic intelligence. Gardner (1984: 207) would perhaps consider Emily's 'bodily motion and capacity to handle' the pram as the core of her body intelligence. Repeating this behaviour will ensure further mastery of body intelligence, again echoing Neisser's (1976: 56) description of schema as 'a pattern of action as well as a pattern for action'.

Observation point:

As you watch children involved in play, do you notice how their schematic interests seem to drive their interests? Do some children display a singular schematic interest? For other children can you observe a combination of schematic interests?

Water: 'Transporting' (23rd June; twenty-five months)

It was mid morning. Emily was outside investigating the water. I was observing her for many minutes before she became aware of my presence. Once noticed, I said hello and asked Emily what she was doing. 'Water, water' Emily responded, as she continued to tip water from the jug to the floor.

I inquired further, 'are you making puddles?' Emily did not respond.

Emily seemed completely absorbed in her actions, using a small jug to repeatedly filling and emptying the water on to the floor. Figure 7.4 illustrates Emily's change of focus as she began tipping the water from the jug into a large bowl. Emily had to refill the jug many times in order to fill the large bowl; she appeared resolute in filling the bowl. Surprisingly when the bowl was accidentally knocked over by another child, Emily seemed unperturbed, showing no outward signs of upset or frustration. Instead she selected a yellow watering can and returned to tipping the water onto the floor. Unsurprisingly it was not long before Emily's attention and concentration once again returned to filling up containers.

Until this point in time it had seemed Emily had used the water as a material to contain and explore dynamic vertical trajectories. Yet looking to the future as the observations of Emily continue over the next period of time, it is conceivable that other possible forms of thought were now being explored. Other 'fine threads' that until this point had perhaps not previously been noticed. I wondered if Emily's interests and motivation also extended to include an interest in transporting?

Figure 7.4 Tipping water

Figure 7.5 Controlling the tap

Figure 7.5 shows how Emily confidently used the tap to access water from the large water butt independently. With care Emily controlled the tap allowing the water to flow from the large water butt to a small blue watering can.

After competently filling the small blue watering can, Emily pours the water from the watering can into the compartment at the back of the car. Carefully she pours the water until the compartment appears full and then proceeds to scoop the water from the compartment at the back of the car and pour it onto the car seat. The water flowed off the seat and dripped onto the floor. Emily stood and watched, as the water appeared to disappear onto the floor.

Returning to the water butt Emily refilled the small blue jug, walked to the sand pit and tipped the water from the jug onto the sand, Emily repeated this activity several more times.

Discussion

It appears Emily's interest with water seems to have moved on. This resonates with Forman's (1994) belief that the physical properties of different mediums can influence children's thinking. Initial observations highlight and link Emily's interest in the medium of water with containing, enveloping and exploring dynamic vertical trajectory movements. For Athey (2007) the fluid properties of water provide a match for Emily's forms of thought, whilst Forman (1994: 38) may propose that the physical property of water 'easily' provides its 'affordance' for containing and transporting (Figures 7.4 and 7.5).

Forman (1994) suggests that different mediums give different messages to children, and explains that the messages are 'biased' depending on the medium from which they originate. This infers that Emily has received such a 'message' and is displaying 'a biased' perspective or view towards the water. Such a view or 'bias' towards the medium of water is seen by Forman (1994) as a 'strength'. Through containing water and investigating insideness, Emily's 'bias' has influenced her thoughts, provoking her to consider that once contained, the water can also be transported. Emily now appears to understand that the physical property of water also 'affords' transporting (Figure 7.7). It is not the water *per se* that is important – rather it is what Emily *can do with* the water that makes for a schematic match.

The language match that practitioners offer is very important. For example, when Julie first began to watch Emily that morning and joined her at the water butt she asked her 'are you making puddles?' Julie noticed that Emily ignored her comment. This is probably because Julie asked a 'content' question – she tried to interpret what she thought Emily was doing rather than match her language to Emily's actions. If Julie had said 'you are tipping the water, it's flowing out' – perhaps Emily would have responded – even echoed some of those words. Practitioners are more likely to make a schematic match with children if they describe their actions rather than impose a content interpretation on them. Recognizing the 'form of thought … the persistent threads of thinking' displayed by the child (Nutbrown 2011: 46) provides a lens into the child's world and an opportunity to match language to actions.

Observation point:

As you watch children involved in play, consider how you reflect on children's actions over time. Do you build up an understanding of their schematic development in the round, and with the passing of time? Consider how this practice might improve knowledge and understanding of their development?

How do children's newly emerging schemas reveal themselves and how do we know that children have moved on to new explorations?

Different media: 'making marks'
(5th July; twenty-seven months)

When I arrive this morning I find Emily sitting on the edge of the indoor sand tray holding a small metal bucket and soup ladle. She has been very still for several minutes, seemingly unaware of the other children or adults in the nursery room. She appeared to be deeply involved and concentrating. Continuing to focus on the sand Emily scooped up a ladle of sand and placed it inside the bucket; she repeated this several more times. Emily's focus seemed to come to an abrupt end, when, without warning she rapidly placed all the equipment back into the sand pit and made her way to the outdoor area, and on her way to the door Emily acknowledged my presence with a smile.

Outdoors she had collected a small clear jug and a small plastic measuring spoon. Standing very still, Emily tipped water from one to the other. Her actions seemed controlled, and she did not to spill any of the water. Moving around the outdoor area to the bridge, Emily placed the measuring spoon on the ground and tipped water into it. This time some water spilled. Emily did not seem concerned by this. Taking the measuring jug and its remaining water she walked across to the blackboard that is fastened to the wall and selected a paintbrush.

Figure 7.6 Making marks with water

Dipping the paintbrush into the water, Emily used the water to make marks on the board (Figure 7.6), mainly using a selection of horizontal and vertical movements to create the marks. When required she replenished the jug with water independently filling it from the water butt. As she continued to use the water to create marks on the blackboard, Emily selected a wooden log to stand on.

Why did Emily choose to stand on the log? Was it to intensify her kinaesthetic sense of height, her vertical trajectory or was it simply to reach higher? Are these marks a representation of the back and forth journeys she makes as she moves around the nursery?

Emily's marks reached to the top of the board. Emily refilled her water supply twice more, each time displaying a strong determination as she marched from the water butt to the blackboard. Emily did not stop until she had covered the whole blackboard with water.

Discussion

Emily appears purposefully and enthusiastically to continue to explore and gain experience with containing and transporting, effectively matching her forms of thought with content from within the indoor and outdoor environment (Athey

2007). Piaget (1959: 283) considers such practical exploits as a prerequisite for 'symbolism and representation'.

Emily's use of vertical and horizontal movements (Figure 7.6) when making marks at the blackboard support Athey's (2007: 78) notion that 'most early marks are a figurative outcome of bodily movement'. This implies that Emily's mark making on the blackboard could be explained as a representation of her continual horizontal back and forth explorations, together with her interest in dynamic vertical trajectories. Yet Nutbrown (2011) demonstrates how a child (Jeanette) represents the actions of containing and enveloping by covering a whole area of paper in one colour. In what can be assumed is a similar representation, Emily uses water to cover and envelope the blackboard. Here Forman's (1994: 38) belief that different media allow children to gain a 'bias' towards their properties suggests the possibility that Emily has discovered yet another new 'affordance' for representing her enveloping forms of thought with the medium of water.

Perhaps on this occasion, Emily's intention is not to make representations of her bodily movements, but to use the water to cover the board. Forman (1994: 38) believes that 'each medium has physical properties that make some concepts more easily represented than others'. Emily's 'affordance' for representing her enveloping forms of thought transforms the water into a covering. If this is the case, Emily could be using the water to represent a symbol (Forman 1994). Standing on the log enables Emily to reach to the top of the board. If Figure 7.6 portrays Emily's intention to 'cover' the whole board, she needs to reach to the top.

If Emily's intention within this activity is to 'cover' the board, it is important to note that this is in contrast to Athey's (2007: 139) findings in the Frobel project, where she states that 'children's symbolic representations, *containing* and *enveloping* [also] came later than the representations of trajectories'. However, if Emily had gained sufficient containing and enveloping experiences, it makes sense that covering marks will also emerge.

Observation point:

As you watch the children in your setting consider, are children provided with opportunities to select their own resources, reflect on their own actions and to wallow in their own thoughts, without adult interrupting?

Do some children demonstrate connections between their physical movements and their mark making?

Filling: 'Figurative representation'
(12th July; twenty-seven months)

Emily was standing outdoors near the water butt with three other children. She waved and smiled at me as I entered the outdoor area. I took this as a cue to become involved with the small group of children. Spending several further minutes filling and emptying different containers of water onto the floor, the children laughed and giggled as it splashed onto my feet and legs.

Emily was very proficient at filling her watering can. She was able to turn on the tap, hold the watering can steady to allow the water to travel through the small hole at the top. Although Emily could not see the water inside the watering can, she obviously understood that it took time for the watering can to fill with water.

After several minutes Emily moved away from the other children to follow her own interests. Using two hands to lift and tip the watering can, Emily was able to aim and direct the flow of water from the spout into a range of preselected containers. Emily's interest also appeared to extend to what was happening inside the watering can, as she regularly took time to pause from her actions to look inside the watering can.

It seemed to me that Emily understood that the amount of water in the watering can was decreasing. Gaining a visual perception of this would strengthen her thoughts and understanding of the concept. After refilling and repeating her exploits with the watering can over the morning, Emily then began to use a combination of chalk and water make marks on the blackboard.

Figure 7.7 Vertical marks

Figure 7.7 shows how Emily used a combination of chalk and her wet fingers to make vertical marks on the board. She only used a downwards motion to make the marks, therefore the marks could have been a figurative representation of the trajectory pattern of the water as it flows from the watering can to the container.

With each activity driving and consolidating the other, the fine threads connecting Emily's intermittent explorations with the water and the mark making activities has become more visible to me and her understanding seems to have strengthened and support given to her in her ongoing development and forms of thought can be of a better match.

Discussion

Gardner (1984) characterizes 'the fine motor movements of one's fingers and hands', together with the 'capacity to work skilfully with objects' with that of evolving (207). Such 'bodily-kinaesthetic intelligence' is evidenced by Emily's proficiency in filling the watering can and controlling the water tap, as she continues to display her resolute enthusiasm and persistence in her quest to explore her forms of thought.

In Emily's frequent checking of the water level, it seems appropriate to propose that Emily has developed an understanding of the relationship between pouring water from the watering can, and the decreasing levels of water in the watering can. In understanding this relationship, Athey (2007: 142) would identify this as a 'functionally dependent relationship'.

The almost imperceptible links between the different content selected and explored by Emily are becoming visible.

- The downward motion of the water as it flows from the water butt into the watering can.
- The vertical movement of the water as it flows from the watering can.
- The downward movement of the water level as it decreases inside the watering can.

Such transparency within Emily's forms of thought means that it is not a surprise when Emily uses the blackboard to make vertical marks. A logical conclusion would be to assume that these are 'figurative representations' of Emily's forms of thought (Athey 2007: 79) and her experience with dynamic vertical trajectory.

It is possible that Emily's real intention with the mark making was to represent the decreasing water level within the watering can. Emily spent time investigating how she could change the water level inside the watering can. Perhaps, when standing at the chalkboard, she also imagined the downward vertical mark to represent the water inside the watering can. There is a potential connection between the linear marks and the decreasing water level. The lines could be a symbolic representation (Athey 2007) of the downward movement of the water level in the jug and in making a downward mark, Emily may well be actively symbolizing the decreasing water. The observation does not include sufficient information; we would need Emily to say something associated with the actions to be certain of the connection. However, such spontaneous use of 'graphic form' (78) continues to suggest that even at such a young age Emily has a perceptual plan to guide her and support her as a social actor in her own learning.

Observation point

When watching children involved in play, do you reflect upon children's varied activities and what might link them together?

Recognizing the fine threads of children's thinking allows us to gain a greater understanding of our young children's true capabilities and how their explorations might be supported.

Enveloping: 'misunderstanding' (14th July; twenty-seven months)

I had not intended to observe Emily today, but when her key worker told me of Emily's reoccurring interest in mark making I decided to watch. Emily's key worker explained that over a ten minute period of time Emily had been using a paint brush and water on the blackboard to make marks. Emily had repeatedly refilled the cup with water to allow her to repaint the marks to ensure they stayed visible. Today Emily seemed to be making curves and ark shapes on the blackboard with the water. I quickly joined Emily at the blackboard and began to narrate what I thought were her actions, believing I was using language to support the actions. 'Emily making marks... big shapes... curved shapes... Emily tipping the water... is the water falling?'

Julie: what are you doing?

Emily: (smiling) 'cover, I cover ... all gone all gone'
Julie: What has gone?
Emily did not respond to the question. She turned her back to me and returned
to the board, continuing with her pursuits of enveloping and covering the board.
Taking this as Emily signalling that she wished to be left alone I did not carry on
the line of questioning and stopped observing her.

Discussion

Atherton and Nutbrown (2013: 37) explain that 'to talk genuinely with children when they play demands a familiarity which can induce recall and enable relaxed probing'. Emily patiently and politely accepted my attempts at narrating her actions. The intention to provide Emily with 'language of form' to help her 'embed conceptual understanding' fell short. Perhaps in haste and excitement Julie misinterpreted Emily's actions, subsequently providing a language accompaniment to support a dynamic trajectory interest when this was not the child's intent. Sometimes we can misinterpret children's meanings, which is why language should match the action – not what we assume to be a child's focus.

Whilst in many situations at only twenty-seven months of age Emily may be viewed as powerless and incapable (Lahman 2008), it is very evident on this occasion that Emily has both control and an understanding of the situation. Her spontaneous reply 'cover, I cover ... all gone all gone' reflects her form of thought, her prominent interest at this moment of time – enveloping (Athey 2007).

Emily's use of 'I' suggests her prevailing control, and her cognitive competence. Emily provides verbal confirmation of her thoughts, her focus. She is not engaging in a social conversation (Piaget 1959), instead her dialogue affords her 'polite departure' (Athey 2007: 252). Julie took Emily's response as her way of informing Julie that her presence was not required, and Julie understood that Emily was both competent and capable of continuing without interference. Fortunately on this occasion Julie's 'tactless out of place comments' (Atherton and Nutbrown 2013: 39) did not deter Emily from her ongoing pursuits, and from her dominant schematic interest at that moment in time. Mismatch can happen but children are often so intent that they are able to continue what they are doing undeterred. With practice, practitioners can hone the skill of matching language to children's actions in order to affirm children's schematic actions and extend their language. If they hear language that matches their intent, they may well repeat those words and phrases because they hold greater meaning for them.

Observation point:

When observing children, do we always gain their permission? Do we acknowledge them as knowledgeable beings from whom we must learn? There are times when children need be to free to explore and experiment without adult involvement or interference.

Environmental resources: 'insideness'
(22nd August; twenty-eight months)

I visited Emily at home, and on my arrival Emily was waiting by the front door, she appeared both pleased and excited by the forthcoming visit.

At the start of the visit I spent some time sharing and reading stories with Emily before asking her if it was ok to take some photographs of her playing. Emily responded positively, smiling and saying 'yes yes yes yes'. Sharing the camera with Emily, together we took a couple of photographs of her toys.

Initially Emily seemed reluctant to play without my input. Eventually with her mum's encouragement Emily became involved with a wooden number jigsaw. The wooden jigsaw had both a number and a picture (an equivalent symbol) from 1–10. The aim of the jigsaw puzzle was to put the correct number symbol by each picture.

As Emily correctly replaced each piece of the puzzle, she said the number name out loud. Emily's mother confirmed, 'she knows the number names. You like 8, 9 and 10 best'. On completion, Emily gestured for me to take a photograph of the jigsaw puzzle.

After a short time Emily's interest turned towards her dolls. She expertly removed the clothes from one before placing it in the fabric carrycot placed on the floor. Emily's mother explained, 'she is always undressing and dressing her dolls, I have to help with the dressing, but the clothes are on and off constantly'.

Emily placed a second doll inside the carrycot, and pulled up the cover to enclose both dolls inside. A few moments later the larger doll was removed from the fabric carrycot and placed inside Emil's toy pram at the other side of the room. Returning to the fabric carrycot Emily placed her feet fully inside it, then bent down onto her knees so she was able to sit completely in it.

Figure 7.8 Sitting inside

As illustrated by Figure 7.8, *Emily sat contentedly within the fabric carrycot, with her feet completely enclosed within the zipped section. Emily sat there smiling for nearly fifteen minutes. Emily sat within the fabric carrycot to have her drink.*

Eventually Emily's focus returned to her doll (redressed by Emily's mother). Emily again removed the clothing and replaced it inside her toy pram, also placing the second doll and the juice cup inside the pram. Emily determinedly and enthusiastically proceeded to push the pram around the room.

Emily pushed the pram around the room, skilfully manoeuvring between the chair and the settee. Emily has an obvious understanding of the space and size of the gap.

Occasionally Emily paused to take a drink before returning to her purposeful and obviously pleasurable endeavour. Emily's mother remarked, 'she is very physical. I noticed this recently at a wedding we went to. At the reception she started dancing, always moving, very natural. She wanted to dance. We could not stop her'.

Without any warning Emily finished pushing the pram, left the sitting room and headed for the stairs, causing her mother to call 'don't play on the stairs' before explaining to me 'she likes the stairs – it's all the time with the stairs'.

Was Emily trying to tell us something? Her constant fascination with the stairs suggests her continual interest in vertical trajectories. Whilst it is not possible to fully understand, it would make sense that after spending nearly twenty minutes pushing a pram and exploring horizontal movements, Emily may now wish to extend and alter her investigation to gain more experience with vertical trajectories. Emily came back into the sitting room, climbed on the settee and began to bounce, saying, 'I bounce'. With a big smile and a cheeky voice Emily's mother says 'You are a scallywag today aren't you?'

Discussion

Emily's initial endeavours display continuity with a containing and enveloping form of thought. Her interest and fascination with the jigsaw reflect consistency in Emily's choices of environmental resources across the home and the nursery. Nutbrown (2011: 38) identifies that consistency across 'experiences and materials' is a pedagogical underpinning of effective early education.

Emily completes the puzzle with ease, whilst also recalling all the number names; at only twenty-seven months of age, Emily can competently recognize and use number names. In this situation Nutbrown (2011) and Athey (2007) would explain that Emily's speech, and her knowledge of number names has arisen from her mother's content based commentary, to support Emily's actions as she repeatedly completes the puzzle. Super and Harkness (2002) would draw links with the mediating and shaping role of family culture suggesting that the home environment and consequently Emily's toys are greatly influenced by individual parental ethno-theories.

Super and Harness's (2002) 'parental ethno-theories' are arguably similar to Nutbrown (2011) and Athey's (2007) uses of the term 'pedagogy', in that they have a significant influence over the culture within the learning environment.

Emily's ease in successfully mastering the skill of number recognition makes sense when considered in relation to her individual fascinations and forms of thought. It would also seem possible that other young children with similar forms of thought would be similarly confident with such number knowledge. Nutbrown (2011) also questions the relevance of prescribed early curricula, suggesting that 'educators can waste time and insult the intellect of young children' (148), and advocating that rather than preparing children for school through the use of a predetermined curriculum, 'Being and behaving as a learner and a thinker is the type of preparation for future learning that children need' (148).

Since Julie's last home visit it was obvious that Emily's skill and competence in navigating the pram around the settee has greatly increased. This verifies Gardner's (1984) belief that to establish a level of 'mastery' requires evolving 'bodily-kinaesthetic intelligence' (207). While agreeing with Gardner's (1984) beliefs, Nutbrown (2011) also points out that through such practical activities, children also gain greater understanding of many mathematical and scientific concepts such as:

> Capacity, tessellation, spatial order, size, shape, height, angles, perimeter, circumference, numbers, sorting, time, matching, quantity, position, estimation, transformation, addition, length, equivalence, distance, symmetry, properties of natural materials, cause, effect and functional relationships, centrifugal forces, rotation, colour, magnetism, gravity, trajectory, natural science, change and speed. (78)

As Emily continues to explore her persistent forms of thought, she too gains greater understanding of mathematical and scientific concepts. This supports the suggestion that it is only through a combination of Emily's cognitive and bodily intelligence that she is able 'to judge the timing, force, and extent of [her] movements and to make necessary adjustments in the wake of this information' as she navigates the pram around the settee (Gardner 1984: 211).

Final thoughts

In this chapter Julie's observations and photographs were used to illuminate how a child's schemas can unfold, grow and adapt into new cognitive structures, providing a greater understanding of the mechanisms of cognitive development within her. Observing Emily over sixteen weeks has provided a unique opportunity to witness both her 'cognitive discomfort' and 'cognitive confidence' (Athey 2007: 51), as she has journeyed on her perceptual plan in an attempt to nourish and grow her schema.

Emily's explorations demonstrate how working with young children in a day care setting is both 'complex and demanding' (Nutbrown 2011: 149), and requires adults who are 'tuned in to young children's thinking, open to their ideas and responsive to their ever-active minds' (149). However, at times, Emily reveals that even this is not enough!

Before Emily is ready to fully engage in learning, she needs to feel socially and emotionally secure. Taking on the apprentice role (Robert 2010), Emily shows how important the key worker is to her emotional security. Only when Emily chooses to venture from this safe and secure base is she ready to fully engage with the business of learning and whilst this is autonomous sometimes, there remains, of course, the need for support and reassurance.

The stories have plotted Emily's cognitive path, as what Piaget (1950) might have called her 'mobile frames', and what we refer to as her schemas, have moved forwards and backwards between motor level, functional dependency and possible symbolic representational level (Athey 2007). Emily's intrinsic drive and her motivation have sensitized her selection and use of environmental resources to match her needs, as materials have revealed new and transforming powers. Emily has reached beyond her present understanding to discover and investigate new and unfamiliar concepts. Emily's story portrays and depicts her as an actor in her own learning.

In the next chapter George's explorations within the nursery and home environment will illustrate his developing 'going through' and 'going around' schemas.

8

George's Going Round a Boundary and Going Through a Boundary Schema

George was twenty-nine months old when the observations started. He attended nursery for three full days each week. George is the oldest child in his family. He has a younger brother, who is about six months old. George lives at home with his younger brother and his mother and father. George's mother was on maternity leave from work when Julie started observing George.

George's transition into nursery at the start of each session could vary, tending to run more smoothly on the days when his best friend arrived before him. On other occasions he was reluctant to let his mother leave. However once settled in nursery, George demonstrated a steely determination within his pursuits.

Water: 'discoveries' (26th April; twenty-nine months)

George was already outdoors and busy in the sand; his attention seemed to be focused on the top of a plant pot. The plant pot was filled to the brim with sand and George seemed very intent on patting the sand down, using both his hands and at times a spade to pat and smooth the sand in line with the brim of the plant pot. George smiled at me seeming to acknowledge my presence, but showed no other signs of interest, quickly returning to his task with the sand and the plant pot.

When the task had been completed to George's satisfaction, he left the sand pit and collected a watering can filled with water. He then began to water the plants that surrounded the wooden playhouse. After pausing to look at the plants, George continued to run his watering can along the window ledge of the playhouse. As he reached the end of the playhouse, George tipped the watering can, allowing the water to flow onto the floor. Continuing to walk, George made a water trail on the floor. The concentration on George's face suggested that this was not an accidental action.

George's actions resemble the familiar actions that would be observed in many children displaying a schematic interest around vertical and horizontal trajectories and containing. Such familiarity can provide an understanding, even a confidence, with regards George's forms of thought. On this occasion such confidence was short-lived.

A large piece of driftwood measuring approximately 1 m in length × 0.5 m width × 0.5 m in height was positioned at the far side of the outdoor area. George displays an obvious interest in the piece of drift wood. Figure 8.1 identifies when George with his water-filled watering can turned his attention to the driftwood and started to pour water into the nooks and holes in its surface.

Figure 8.1 illustrates how with obvious care and attention to detail George attempted to tip water into the small hollows and nooks of the bark. Rather than randomly tipping the water, George appeared to consider and plan where to place the water. It appeared he was methodically moving around the outer circumference of the log, seeking out the nooks and spaces he could fill with water.

Throughout his investigation of the log George selected and used a variety of resources from which he was able to tip and pour water. Each time George had

Figure 8.1 The driftwood log

to stop to refill the container, he continued his investigation from his previous finishing place.

Close observation of this investigation revealed the incredible and astonishing high level of accuracy displayed by a child only twenty-nine months old. George appeared unperturbed when the water seemed to disappear into the log, suggesting his interest and focus might not be simply containing?

Were George's actions indicating that he had other schematic interests?

Were my initial ideas and confidence with regards to George's interest around trajectories and containing schemas somewhat hasty?

Indoors at the end of the morning, George sat on the carpet area listening to a story. Interestingly he positioned himself inside a large plastic hulahoop. As he listened to the story, George moved the hoop up and down the core of his body, raising it above his head, then meticulously down the length of his body. George repeated this many times throughout the whole of the story time session.

Was George using the hoop as a boundary? Is he going through the hoop? Is he going through a boundary? It appeared George could be using the hoop to continue an exploration of 'going through'.

Discussion

Atherton and Nutbrown (2013: 139) maintain that 'the ability to discern children's forms of thinking as they play requires important insight'. However, they warn that in providing an 'appropriate accompaniment in learning', the accompaniment may need to be adjusted and modified 'in the light of what is seen and heard'. It seems appropriate to suggest George's actions with the sand and the watering of the plants provided evidence of an interest in containing, and in dynamic vertical trajectory. Further evidence of such forms of thought was gained through conversations and photographs of George's earlier experiences at home. George's patterns of action and behaviour at this moment in time were, we suggest, the result of his former experiences.

Through pursuing a combination of forms of thought, experiences are 'treated or modified in such a way as to become incorporated into the structure ... In other words, every newly established connection is integrated into an existing schematism' (Piaget and Inhelder 1969: 5). Nutbrown (2011) professes that perceiving and gaining insight into young children's thinking can only be gained through observation, reflection and a willingness to question. As George placed objects inside containers he gained the opportunity to observe the rim, the neck, the boundary of the container, whilst the dynamic trajectory of the object entering the container offered George an opportunity to observe the object going through the boundary. It is through the coordination of George's 'simple early behaviours' of containing and trajectory that a 'more complex understanding' of going through a boundary has evolved (Athey 2007: 152). This is a form of thought that has become more evident in later observations of George's investigations and discoveries.

George's action of passing the hoop over his head would be classified in Athey's (2007: 149) analysis as a 'motor level' example of going through a boundary. Other such examples would include 'pushing nails through clay', and 'pushing one thing through another'. If George were attempting to pour water into and through the boundary of log, this would also be considered as a motor level. Whilst it is not plausible to know his thoughts, his systematic and logical process suggests a higher cognitive level. It is possible that George may have been thinking 'in this hole the water disappears, it has gone through, in this hole it remains, it is inside.' This implies that George's understanding of 'going through' is functionally dependent on passing through the boundary (Athey 2007). The power of Georges actions also lies in the knowledge that he was in control of deciding what to do and part of his thinking might also be 'I did that'.

George can be described as being both physically and mentally active as he explored the log and, for Atherton and Nutbrown (2013), 'essential practical endeavour' forms the foundation of future mathematical knowledge (67) and an opportunity to 'germinate' (49) future understanding of concepts, such as size, width, height, volume, perimeter, distance and circumference. Such a view resonates with Dowling's (2013: 2) beliefs about young children's ability to think: 'thinking is closely linked to early physical and sensory experiences', and we take this to mean that young children's thinking is enhanced through supporting the whole child. Such a view has implications for the development of appropriate pedagogy, learning interactions and curricula for young children.

Observation point:

Socrates said: 'Wisdom begins with wonder.' As young children generate their own learning theories through their wonder about the world around them, so their practitioners must take time to ponder and really consider children's actions and the meaning they convey. It is important not to rush to interpretations about what underpins children's actions because sometimes we can get it wrong and perhaps it is important to be aware that a little knowledge may be a hindrance rather than help?

Water: 'Going through' (10th May; thirty months)

George was in the outdoor area. After saying hello I asked George if I could take some photographs of him this morning. George was pleased with this, and initially came to look at the photographs, until gradually his interest in what he was doing took over and he seemed to forget about the camera.

George and his friend were tipping and pouring water from containers into the black guttering attached to the wall as seen in Figure 8.2. They watched the water as it flowed along the guttering pipe, travelling from the top level to the lower level of the guttering. Initially the water splashed onto the ground when it reached the end of the guttering. After a few moments George positioned a bowl at the end of the guttering to catch and contain the water as it poured out of the guttering (see Figure 8.2).

The water had a bubble solution added to it, and as the water was tipped and poured the amount of bubbles seemed to increase. Perhaps the bubbles in the water helped George to see the patterns the water made as it travelled through and out of the guttering.

The bubbles in the water attracted several other children, who were interested in tipping the water onto the floor and jumping in the puddles they made. The excess water from the puddles began to flow under the gate and down the slope of the

Figure 8.2 Catching the water

nursery drive. Through the spaces in the metal gates the children were able to view the water as it travelled down the drive of the nursery. It did not take long before the flow of the water through the gates and down the incline of the drive attracted George's attention.

Moving from the guttering, George began to tip the water through the spaces in the metal gates. He repeated this many times seeming to watch the water as it made its path down the nursery drive. George's excitement at this discovery was immense. He brought different staff members to watch as he repeated the task for each of them. The adults responded by narrating that the water was going through the gates, supporting George's visual experience and forms of thought.

Later in the morning, when George went inside to get dry, he became engrossed with a set of small wooden curtain hoops. George placed the small wooden hoops one by one onto his extended (right) arm. Keeping his arm very straight, he moved the hoops up to the top of his arm close to his shoulder. The adult sitting close by narrated George's actions 'Your arm goes through the hoops... your arm goes through the round shape of the hoop... your arm is inside the hoop'. George made no verbal response, continuing instead to take the hoops off one by one. George remained interested in the hoops for over ten minutes.

Selecting some wooden blocks that were scattered nearby on the floor, George built a construction that had an open circular shape in the centre. I observed as he moved his fingers forwards and backwards through the circular space. George's fine threads of thought seem to lead him to discover materials and objects that move and/or allow movement from one boundary to another. George's actions and investigations seem to indicate a developing and continuing interest in 'going through'.

Discussion

George began the morning observing the trajectory movement of the water along the guttering. He seemed to display an understanding that a constant flow of water through the guttering was 'functionally dependent' (Athey 2007) on more water being added to the start of the guttering. George maintained the supply of water through the guttering. If viewed alone, this observation could be considered as the endeavour of a child with a dynamic trajectory and/ or containing interest. It is only through the adjustment and modification of insight (Atherton and Nutbrown 2013) that the less obvious forms of thought begin to reveal themselves.

Piaget and Inhelder's (1969) theory would lead us to argue that it is from the coordination of actions, of keeping the water flowing, that George determined that the water was passing from one boundary to another, from the jug to the guttering, and from the guttering to the floor. When George positioned the bowl on the floor, this could be viewed as a 'containing' action, or the movement of the water from the guttering pipe to the bowl could be seen as another boundary for the water to pass through. Through the actions of exploring, containing and enveloping children are able to learn 'about the relationship of going through' (Atherton and Nutbrown 2013: 145). George's apparent switching between different forms of thought could be considered as part of his 'long apprenticeship' (Piaget 1953: 320), as he continues to coordinate his understanding of going through a boundary with other notions. As children develop their schematic knowledge, the connections between schemas often become more apparent.

George attempts to share his discoveries with different adults who respond to his interests by providing related vocabulary to match and extend his interest.

Nutbrown (2011: 70) considers that 'extending and developing children's learning through identifying, understanding, supporting and extending their patterns of thinking' is an essential part of the adult role. With an adult alongside providing a speech representation of his actions, George's exploration indoors with the wooden rings and building bricks can be seen to further strengthen his notions of space, shape underpinned by 'going through' actions.

Without the accompaniment of language, George's exploration would be considered as a motor level activity. Constructing a wooden circular structure immediately after experiencing the actions of going through the hoop could however suggest that George used the bricks to represent the shape of the hoop. A simple representation of the circular shape would also be considered as a motor level.

Alternatively, considering George's previous lived experiences with the water, we can speculate as to whether George was representing his explorations with the water in the guttering; was he using his arm to represent the water as it flows through the boundary of the gate? When language is not invented by the child but transmitted in 'ready made, compulsory, and collective forms' (Piaget and Inhelder 1969), it cannot be used by the child for self-expression. Instead, the child 'needs a means of self expression, that is a system of signifiers constructed by him and capable of being bent to his wishes' (58). One interpretation could be that George used the hoops and his arm to 'relive the event', the movement of the water through the boundary of the gate (60). If this were the case, George's use of the wooden rings would be considered as a symbolic representation. It is such fine observations and reflections over time that help to identify possible connections between seemingly unrelated episodes.

Observation point;

When you watch children involved in play, do you ever underestimate young children's capabilities? Do they sometimes surprise you with their explorative play? Consider looking more closely – and over time – at young children's continuing fascinations, what can you learn?

Such observations, when shared and discussed with colleagues can form an important part of practitioner's own continuing professional development and enhance the learning experiences of young children.

Sand: 'Going through' (19th May; thirty months)

George was sitting alone in the sand area apparently placing sand inside a cardboard tube which was about 10 cm in diameter and 30 cm long. He looked up and smiled at me before quickly returning his focus on the tube. Exploring the tube he placed his hand and full arm into the tube. At one point George managed to put his full arm up to his shoulder inside the tube. George proceeded to fill the tube with sand. At times he would pause, appearing to look inside the tube, at other times I observed him reaching into the tube with his whole arm.

George was very engrossed, seeming not to even acknowledge when his best friend had joined him in the activity. George's persistence and involvement in this activity lasted for an extended period of time, unlike his friend, who seemed to quickly loose interest. After observing George's actions for a while, it became evident that he was placing a combination of sand and shells inside the tube. Due to the size and shape of the shells they were becoming lodged inside the tube, so enabling George to fill the tube.

Figure 8.3 depicts George's actions as he lifted up the filled tube and began to shake it, causing the contents of the tube to drop out. Gradually, with each shake, the contents revealed themselves as they fell from the tube.

Emptying the tube required vigorous force, as many of the shells were large and had become caught up with each other. This did not seem to deter George. He seemed as interested in emptying the tube as he was in filling it, indicating that perhaps his interest was in the resources moving through the tube. Once empty, George repeated this activity again. George spent most of the morning, over an hour involved in this activity.

Figure 8.3 Emptying the contents from the tube

At the end of the morning as George was on his way to the bathroom, he noticed the table set up with paper and pens. George became involved with a short episode of mark making. Holding a coloured pen whilst walking around the edge of the table, George was able to use the pen to make a line around the edge of the paper. His key worker confirmed that he often did this. As George moved around the table he left pen marks around the edge of the paper. After several trips around the table George had left a visual boundary of pen marks around the paper. George's mark making and his experiences in the outdoors both display evidence of travelling around the edge and going around a boundary.

Discussion

Unlike sensorimotor intelligence that Athey (2007: 50) likens 'to a slow motion film in which all the pictures are seen in succession, but without fusion', George's schematic interests, his experiments and experiences seem to be beginning to fuse together through the process of 'coordination and connection' (Nutbrown 2011: 30). George seems to be developing a more complex comprehension of the environment. As pursuit of new schemas gives rise to the development of new concepts, George's use of the open-ended materials in his nursery environment becomes sensitized (Atherton and Nutbrown 2013) to match his newly developing *forms of thought*. He seems to manipulate the materials he finds in ways which allow him to further extend his schematic interest.

George's use of the sand and tubes does not appear to be a simple containing investigation. Because of the objects he chooses to fill and empty, we can infer that such a filling and emptying focus appears to be fuelled by an interest in 'going through'. Piaget and Inhelder (1969: 66) identify topology as 'children's first spatial intuitions', a view also held by Athey (2007: 148), who found that the experience of 'going through' provided children with 'elementary topological space notions'. When placing his hand, and then his arm within the tube, George experienced both a 'physical and mental activity' (Atherton and Nutbrown 2013: 139) regarding the shape and notion of space. Nutbrown (2011) clarifies that explorations of containing and 'going through' provide young children with practical mathematical experiences such as shape, size, rotation and space. George's knowledge and his mathematical understanding of the shape and space within the tube is founded on his previous first-hand experiences, as well as his action and motor level encounters.

Did George understand that his arm was bigger and longer than the shells he selected? If his arm will easily pass through the tube, so should the shells. George's actions in shaking the tube were not uncontrolled, nor displaying any form of frustration when trying to get the shells out of the tube. In contrast, George's vigour in shaking out the contents of the tube (Figure 8.3) displays his understanding that the shells *will* come out, it appears that he expects them to travel through the tube just as the water flowed through the pipe outside. Does he now have a theory that objects which are open at each end will allow other (smaller) objects to pass through them? George could be said to be involved in a process of constructing and hypothesizing in an attempt to understand and 'figure out the nature of material objects in the world' (Gardner 1984: 18). As George increases his 'elementary topological space notions' (Athey 2007: 148), his previous experiences with dynamic trajectories seem to now enable him to visualize the movement of the shells through the tube. If 'thought consists of internalized and coordinated action schemas' (Piaget 1959: 357), George is developing his own new 'systems of thought' (Athey 2007: 153) as his schemas coordinate.

In the absence of words and with no clear understanding of what George was thinking – or indeed whether he was seeking to represent anything with his marks – his endeavours at mark making can only be as a figurative representation of his sensorimotor movements (Piaget and Inhelder 1956). Over time, as more insight into George's thinking is gained, and as his own language developed, these ideas may need to be adjusted and modified 'in the light of what is seen and heard' (Atherton and Nutbrown 2013: 139).

For Athey (2007: 50) 'as schemas are coordinated into more and more complex amalgamations the environment is comprehended at a higher level', for George this means that as he continues to find content which he can use to match to his new more complex forms of thought, he developed new understandings and more complex ideas and theories. Through his busyness, and his daily explorations in the real world, George's intrinsic schematic motivation has become the driving force behind his learning. At the age of thirty months, George can already be considered as a confident and capable actor in his own learning (Nutbrown 2011).

Observation point:

As you watch children involved in play, consider how children are manipulating the materials to develop their mathematical and scientific content. What personal theories are they developing and trying to test out through repeated actions with different materials?

How can such explorations and newly developing understandings be recognized, supported and extended?

Cars: 'Movement' (11th June; thirty-one months)

George was at home, busy playing with his garage on the living room floor. George seemed undeterred by my presence. Showing him the camera I sought his permission to take photographs of him while he played.

George placed several of his toy cars in a row on the road of the toy garage. Once in position, George moved his hand and allowed the cars to freely travel down the slope. George seemed interested in the movement of the cars in a downward trajectory. One at a time he pushed the cars back up the slope before letting them roll down again. George repeated this many times.

Next George became interested in his 'Thomas the tank engine' train which he could make the train travel along the carpet. When he pulled the train backwards, the mechanism within the train independently moved it forwards. The train travelled across the carpet until it hit the cupboard. This seemed to please George, as he smiled and laughed. George also repeated this many times.

Eventually George's focus returned to the garage. He seemed to have noticed that some of the features were missing. George competently slotted in a parking sign which formed an arch over the road. Before sending a car down the road and under the archway (created by the parking sign) George slid his arm under the archway and down the road. George selected another car, placing it at the top of the slope he watched the car as it travelled down the road and through the arch and then repeated this action several more times.

From his box of toys, George selected a plastic archway that was not part of the garage. He placed this at the top of the garage and then proceeded to send cars through it. George's focus and his thoughts appeared to have moved on from isolated and simple trajectory movements and his addition of the arches enabled George to also create and experience 'going through' movements. George seemed to have combined his interest and understanding to initiate new experiences and understanding.

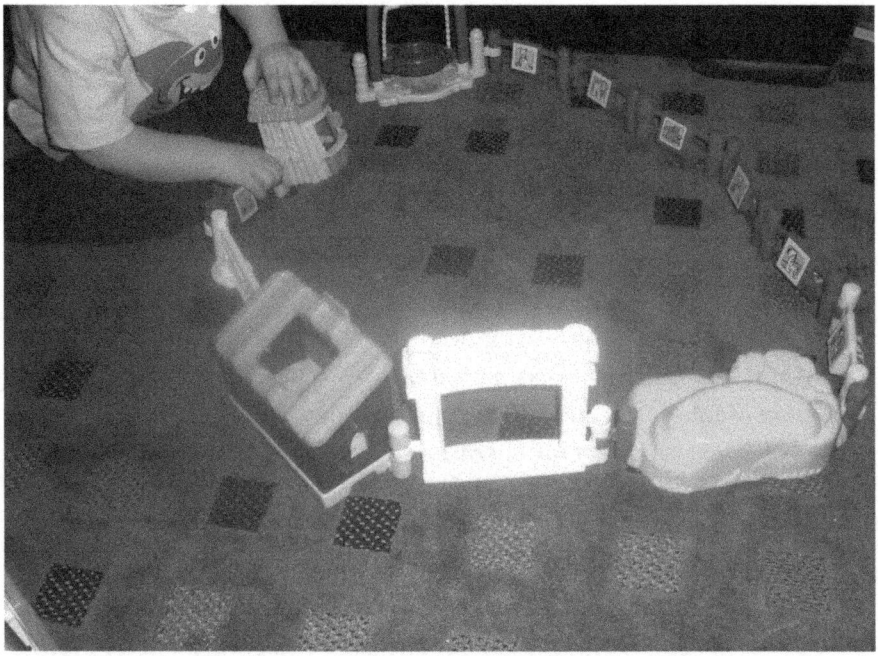

Figure 8.4 Increasing size

At home George's toys are organized into collections and stored in boxes. With a little help from his mother, George put away the cars and the garage and selected the farm set to play with.

I found it interesting that whilst George selected the farm set to play with, he displayed no interest in the farm animals. His whole focus was directed at the farm fence. One piece at a time he began to fix the fence panels together, it took obvious skill and perseverance to complete this task. George spent a further twenty minutes occupied with building and connecting the fence piece together as shown in Figure 8.4. When completed, the fence appeared to resemble a circular boundary shape. Initially George erected it around himself, before moving outside of it. Once all the fence pieces had been used, George added other farm pieces to the fence panels thus continuing to increase the size of the circular structure (Figure 8.4). It took George over thirty minutes to complete the structure. George's mother explained that he enjoys building the fence but that he does not really play with the farm.

Discussion

George's initial activities with the cars suggest further exploration of motor level dynamic trajectory schema, fitting with 'notion of schemas revisited' (Nutbrown's 2011: 29). Whilst George does not seem to be revisiting these schemas at higher level, it may be that through revisiting he is able to continue his 'long apprenticeship' (Piaget 1953: 320), clarifying and consolidating his understanding of 'the nature of material objects in the world' (Gardner 1984: 18).

When 'operations that can be carried out in the head' are initiated from 'sensory and perceptual information accompanying motor actions' (Athey 1990: 70) new and extended learning can take place. This observation provides evidence of George's continuing interest in 'going through' and his actions suggest that he could be testing his 'notions' of shape and space, and his 'topological' knowledge (Athey 2007: 148) by using his arm. Such physical explorations can provide a child with strong perceptual feedback, which in this case enabled George to successfully accommodate and assimilate information into his forms of thought, his 'going through' schema. Johnson (1987: 19) argued that schemas are 'embodied patterns of meaningfully organized experiences' and so an 'image schemata' exist as 'structures that organize our mental representation' (23). If we apply this to George, we anticipate that as he continues to experience, to feel and to gain an embodied perception of 'going through', he will continue to develop his internalized understanding of 'going through' as he builds more content into his pursuit of that schema.

If George's pursuit of his schema is helping to increase his perceptual understanding of 'going through', he will be developing a deeper and richer understanding through using his bodily (kinaesthetic) perception, reinforcing Neisser's (1976: 56) proposal that 'schema is a pattern of action, as well as a pattern for action'.

George's persistent interest in constructing the fence could be evidence of his containing and enveloping interest and Atherton and Nutbrown's (2013: 139) suggestion of adjusting and modifying ideas 'in the light of what is seen and heard' resonates with this observation. If George's form of thinking was containing, there is an expectation that he would place objects within the constructed space. George persisted in what was an obviously tricky job of connecting the panels together, yet he seemed uninterested in using the construction as a container or in order to contain. It appeared that George constructed a three-dimensional representation of a boundary, forming an enclosure, which indicates an interest in the relationship of 'surrounding'.

Whilst it is possible to assume that George's interest in boundaries and surrounding has occurred through the coordination of his schemas, we do not yet know how, at this point, George understands three-dimensional space. An interpretation of these actions could be that George's interest in surrounding is 'simpler' and not the coordination of 'the three topological space schemas: surrounding, enclosure and going through' (Athey 2007: 136). This suggests that through his actions, George is building on his previous experiences and expertise, his 'long apprenticeship' (Piaget 1953: 320) so that what is 'known' leads to what becomes 'better known' (Athey 2007: 51).

Observation point:

When you watch the children in your setting, are you aware of adjusting and modifying your ideas and understanding of young children's 'in the light of what is seen and heard' (Atherton and Nutbrown 2013: 139)? How can continual interpretation and reflection support schematic pedagogy and lead to better understanding of children's coordination of schemas?

Indoors: 'Pushing' (22nd June; thirty-one months)

George did not seem interested in being with his friends, who were all outside. Instead George was indoors where a large empty floor space had been created in which he was freely playing with a selection of balls. He spotted me seeming eager to tell me 'I have balls… I can do big push'. He then proceeded to roll the balls across the floor towards me, and I reciprocated by rolling the balls back to him. This was repeated several times; I began to narrate the actions of the balls as they rolled: 'ball coming to George… I give it a big push… the ball is rolling toward George… George stop the red ball'. George said the colour of each ball as he expertly rolled them back; occasionally he said, 'it's a big push'.

As George attempted to stop a ball using his foot, it rolled between his legs. This seemed to provide George with a new direction of play and exploration. Seeming to forget about me, George attempted to roll the balls through his legs (Figure 8.5). George seemed captivated – mesmerized – by this new experience, seeming to forget about the game he was previously playing. I decided not to redirect or interrupt this new interest, instead I watched him explore and discover how it felt to roll the ball through his legs and under his body. Like Atherton and Nutbrown

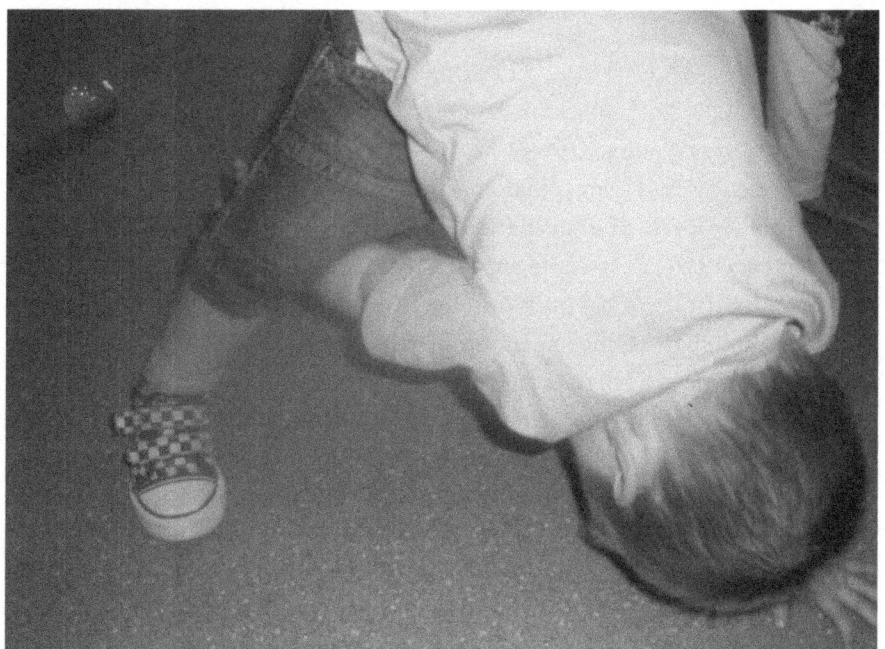

Figure 8.5 Rolling through

(2013: 158) I believed that in order to better 'come to know' George it was important to recognize such opportunities. Once again George had demonstrated his competence in extending his dynamic trajectory interest into a 'going through experience'.

Later in the morning George joined a small group of children at a black builders tray filled with flour. With little hesitation George began to fill a small container with flour, but after a few minutes his interest changed. George placed a smaller container inside the first container – his action seemed quite deliberate; it fitted perfectly with the two rims becoming parallel. George appeared to explore this several more times, placing the smaller container in and out.

George returned to his initial interest, filling the containers with flour. Once full to the rim, George pushed a finger into the centre of the container pushing the flour tightly together, when he removed his finger a small hole remained. Gently and cautiously George pressed his finger into the flour in the builders tray. He appeared almost spellbound, as he recognized that he could use his fingers to make other marks in the flour. Taken together, George used the flour to: fill a small container with flour, make a hole in the centre, place this container in the centre of his circular flour marks. This morning George's experiences involved creating a boundary within a boundary within a boundary.

Discussion

From being very young, George has been interested in exploring how balls behave. Sensory and perceptual information accompanying motor actions leads to higher levels of understanding (Atherton and Nutbrown 2013; Athey 2007; Nutbrown 2011). It would appear now that George is able to recognize the relationship between 'a big push' and the distance the ball travels, implying his understanding that the movement of the ball is functionally dependent on the force and the type of push the ball is given (Athey 2007). George's accompanying language suggests that he is able to anticipate the movement of the ball before it happens; perhaps he plans this. He understands that a 'big push' will cause the ball to travel far before he actually carries out the action. His 'internalized and coordinated action schemas' suggest that George is able to carry out this thinking in his head before he completes the action (Piaget 1959: 357).

In using his legs to form a boundary through which the ball can travel, George can be said to be creating his own continuities, affording further opportunity to explore, think and learn, and to test his ideas of functional dependency (Nutbrown 2011). George's schema depicts him as an actor in his learning journey. George's own intrinsic schematic motivation becomes 'a pattern for action' (Neisser 1976: 56), allowing George the opportunity to retest his understanding. George's speech could be taken as evidence that he seems to understand the functional dependency relationship between his push of the ball and the distance travelled.

George's actions illustrate (Nutbrown 2011: 46) the belief that 'schemas can be considered at the core of children's developing mind'. George has his own perceptual plan to support his learning, of age. Many would find it hard to accept that, at only thirty-two months of age, George is able systematically to plan and select content from the environment which match his forms of thought. Nutbrown (2011: 46) affirms that children's 'threads of thinking' 'connect different areas of content', meaning that George's selection of environmental content is not haphazard or a coincidence, but based on an informed and systematic cognitive plan.

George's play with the flour and containers might be considered to reveal his coordinated schematic explorations; his actions of containing flour and containers within each other suggest a schema of containing and enveloping (Atherton and Nutbrown 2013). His evident interest in the rim of both containers suggests that he is learning about the relationship of going through the boundary, and about putting things inside. Pushing his finger into the flour might be considered to be a further motor level example of going through (Athey 2007).

In considering George's attempt to use the flour to make graphical marks, Athey (2007) reminds us that 'most early marks are figurative outcomes of bodily movements' (78). However, it is plausible from George's previous experiences with coloured pencils and constructing a boundary, to consider that George is now using the marks in the flour to represent a boundary. It may an be 'erroneous characteristic' (Atherton and Nutbrown 2013: 49) of George's thinking, to further speculate that George's going through and surrounding schemas are coordinating, thus crediting George with advancing 'topological space notions' (Athey 2007: 148) and leading to an exploration and interest in concentric boundaries. This is a possibility confirmed by George's mother as she describes his developing interest and knowledge of shapes: 'Yes he knows all shape names, he knows everything, all the shape names, he just remembers them and uses them when he plays.'

Observation point;

When you watch children involved in play, what clues do they provide for you about their learning? How do you listen and act upon them?

What accompanying language do children use which matches their self-directed explorations? How have children come to know abstract language? Do you match children's actions with a verbal accompaniment?

The log: 'Going through' (5th July; thirty-two months)

Many staff members had noted George's fascination with the log, observing him spending time each day investigating the log through pouring water into it.

The following observation took place over a twenty-minute period when George was continuing his daily exploration of the log. I observed as George meticulously and methodically selected a variety of containers, which he used to pour small and precise amounts of water into the hollows of the log. Several times George paused from pouring water into the log; Figure 8.6 illustrates how

Figure 8.6 Pushing fingers into the hollows of the log

George's investigation included pushing his fingers into the hollows of the drift wood.

Such perseverance and detail cannot be incidental. It suggests that George was testing and hypothesizing as he continued his fastidious investigation of the log.

Discussion

George's 'going through' schema appears to continue to drive his actions (Neisser 1976). His perceptual plan for cognitive continuity involves exploration, repetition, mastery and revision. George can see the hollows and holes in the log. Perhaps he pushed his finger in to check where the water was, and in doing so he generated a stronger perceptual feel; he poured water in, and he watched the water disappear. Through such play children gain 'powerful tools for making sense of the world' (Wood and Attfield 2005: 122).

George's motor level actions show considerable persistence, and his level of involvement (Laevers 1976) infers a high level of learning. The complexity of George's thinking cannot be underestimated, as 'mathematics it seems is never far away from young children's actions' (Nutbrown 2011: 86). Through the physical and mental involvement of this activity George is gaining early and valuable experience of concepts such as size, shape, position, height, speed and equivalence. Opportunities for such discovery are vital, not only to build the foundations of mathematical understanding but also to support children's dispositions and inclination for life-long learning (Moyles 2010).

Observation point:

When watching young children involved in play do you try to recognize and acknowledge their dispositions for learning?

How do you highlight and share this important information with parents? And what opportunities are there for parents to similarly share with practitioners what they have noticed about their children's play and learning?

Going through; 'Hypothesizing'
(12th July; thirty-two months)

As I observed George's investigations with the log this morning, something seemed a little different.

Initially the morning started as previously, as observed in Figure 8.1 George explored the log by pouring water into the hollows of the log. After a short time George's exploration started to follow a different path. Still keeping his whole attention focused on the log, George began to walk around the perimeter of the driftwood. He repeated this three times. I continued to observe, intrigued as to what he was doing. Gradually I realized he may be looking for the water? I posed a question:

Julie: 'Where has the water gone?'

George made no verbal response. Instead he ran away and quickly returned with a bucket. George placed the bucket on the ground next to the log.

(Amazed) Julie: 'What is the bucket for?'

George stood and looked at me, replying: 'for the water, I get the water'.

From the tone in George's voice such an assumption seemed obvious. It seemed George's intention was to collect the water in the bucket, just as he had previously done with the guttering (Figure 8.2). George's previous experiences had led him to believe the water would pass through the log in order to be captured in the bucket. At thirty-two months George was demonstrating a high level of abstract thinking. Figure 8.7 depicts George waiting for the water to come out from the log.

Figure 8.7 Recapturing the water

Unfortunately he was unsuccessful in recapturing any water into the bucket this morning.

As the outdoor area became busy with other children, George seemed to lose his focus and became involved in a chasing game with his friends. Interestingly it involved chasing around the boundary of the outdoor environment.

Later in the morning I observed George, as he explored the sand indoors.

George had a funnel. He tipped sand into the funnel and watched as it flowed out. George was able strategically to place resources to catch the sand as it flowed through the funnel.

George repeated his actions many times, seeming to test and retest his ideas and understanding. He watched the sand as it flowed from the bottom of the funnel.

George observed the sand inside the funnel as it flowed out.

Figure 8.8 illustrates George as he watches the sand travel through and out of the funnel. I closely observed George for nearly ten minutes before asking:

Julie: Where is the sand?

George made no verbal response.

Julie: Does the sand go through the funnel?

George pointed to the sand pit replying 'I catch the sand'.

Figure 8.8 Retesting

As an observer the use of a schema provides a foundation from which we can 'come to know' young children's thoughts (Atherton and Nutbrown 2013: 58). It is possible George was pondering why the water and the log do not behave in a similar way to the funnel and the guttering? We can only admire George as he attempts to make sense of such a complex world.

Discussion

Through his extended explorations it is possible that George has recognized 'patterns and relationships' within the log (Wood and Attfield 2005: 122). If such an assumption is correct it is also plausible to believe George has gained understanding of the functional dependency relationship between water going in and coming out; this could be part of his developing theory about how water behaves. Athey (1990: 70) argues that children's understanding of functional dependencies 'arises from the application of earlier schematic behaviours'. George's previous motor level experiences of containing and going through a boundary may have afforded his theory that 'what goes in will also come out'. If he pours water in, experience has shown him that it will pass through and then reappear. But the log is behaving differently – his theory about water does not hold up when he tests it with the log, no matter how much water he pours in – nothing comes out. From a mathematical perspective George is gaining an understanding of capacity and conservation, and the seeds of scientific discoveries around the properties of water and wood are being sewn.

Piaget and Inhelder (1969: 20) identify reversibility as the source of 'future operations of thought', explaining 'the most immediate result of the reversibility structure is the formation of notions of conservation'. It is becoming more apparent through the coordination of schemas that George is experiencing (even if not fully understanding and articulating) several higher order concepts. George's actions could also be considered as illustrating Piaget's (1959: 357) notion that 'thought consists of internalized and coordinating action schemas'. In placing the bucket to 'get the water', George has demonstrated his theory that (as with other water and pouring experiences) he should be able to collect the water.

Athey (2007: 192) considers knowledge as an 'end point', identifying that it is produced through a continuum from 'struggle to playfulness'. It distinguishes children's 'desire to master some perceived problem' as the starting point, the 'struggle'. George's fascination with the log initiates his problem; possibly stemming from his developing functional dependency understanding of water passing through a boundary. Whilst it is not possible to be categoric about our interpretation of George's thinking, it would seem that he considers it to be possible to recontain the water as it exits the log, hence his placing of a bucket. Athey's (2007: 192) notion of 'struggle' resonates with Neisser's (1976: 56) 'pattern for action' as both can be considered as intrinsic self-motivation.

It is also possible to consider that when George is not able to recontain the water, the reversibility of his action to recollect the water (Piaget and Inhelder 1969), George experiences a level of 'cognitive discomfort' (Athey 2007: 51), an emotion he seems to demonstrate – and deal with – in his behaviour by quickly leaving the activity.

George's intrinsic motivation, his 'struggle' (Athey 2007: 192) and his 'pattern for action' (Neisser 1976: 56) reappear later in the nursery. Possibly as an attempt to clarify and consolidate his understanding of 'the nature of material objects in the world' (Gardner 1984: 18), George matches content to his thoughts on passing through a boundary with his use of the sand. This verifies Nutbrown's (2011: 46) view that 'children's persistent threads of action ... involves children creating their own continuities in the process of exploring, thinking and learning'. It may be that through such continuities George is able to continue his 'long apprenticeship' (Piaget 1953: 320), clarifying and consolidating his understanding of mathematical concepts and 'the nature of material objects in the world' (Gardner 1984: 18) and evidenced by high level and repeated motor level explorations.

Observation point:

As you watch children involved in play, do you recognize and acknowledge young children's learning as they pass through the continuum from 'struggle to playfulness' (Athey 2007: 192)? What continuities of action, speech, graphic and thought representations do you see? How can you support children by further extending their interests with meaningful and challenging content?

Going around: 'Journeying' (14th July; thirty-one months)

George waved and shouted hello when he spotted me this morning.

He appeared very focused in his journeying around the outdoor area. Gliding on the bike, running on his feet and pushing the pram all provided a different experience and perhaps a new discovery for George this morning.

When George noticed the bubbles in the water, his physical focus changed. Scooping bubbles into a small jug, George's movements became much slower and more precise, he appeared to be using the bubbles to leave a trail around the outdoor area. He walked slowly around the outdoor area tipping bubbles from the jug onto the ground. This action left a distinct trail, a record of his journey around the space of the outdoor area. From time to time George looked back and around at the trail of bubbles he had left. Was George trying to use the bubbles to record his path, to provide a visual representation of his journey around the space? Or was this a happy accident?

Later in the morning I observed George standing at the blackboard using a wet sponge to make marks on the board. George covered the whole of the blackboard with his marks.

Discussion

Nutbrown (2011: 42) argues that the curriculum for younger children, such as those of George's age, needs 'careful consideration' with a 'clear understanding of what is meant by continuity and progression'. George's involvement and his busyness imply that he has his own ideas about continuity and progression, which the environment rich in open-ended materials allows him to pursue. According to Nutbrown's (2011) interpretation George can be said to have previously demonstrated continuity through his 'persisted threads of action, representation, speech and thought' (46).

Following on from Atherton and Nutbrown's (2013: 145) view that the 'going through' behaviours of Gregg, a child in their study developed from a coordination of his containing and enveloping schema, it is logical to assume that George's behaviour of exploring boundaries is as a result of the coordination of his dynamic trajectory and containing schemas. George appears to confidently and capably match his threads of thought through a variety of environmental content. His use of the bike, the pram and running to explore the boundary of the outdoor environment are all examples of this.

Making the journey in different ways and on different modes (bike, pram and running) provided George with additional kinaesthetic information. Gardner (1984) and Johnson (1987) state that by using different bodily motions to explore, perceptual understanding can be increased. This means that it is plausible to argue that by travelling around on the bike, George gained a different understanding of the speed it takes to traverse the circumference of the area. By pushing the pram, George may become more aware of the bumps and lumps on the floor due to the pram's poor suspension. Without language, Athey (1990: 68) would perhaps consider that George's various journeys around the outdoor area 'do not appear to have representational significance' and would characterize them as motor level actions. Such motor level experiences add to George's 'database' of the underpinning schematic behaviour and offer different forms of 'feedback' to him as a learner and explorer.

In light of George's previous use of content to represent boundaries, we can view his actions with the bubbles as a further continuity of his thought (Nutbrown 2011). This makes it conceivable to suggest that the bubbles represent his journey around the outdoor area, though we can't know this to be the case so we must see George's bubble trail and his marks on the blackboard as further examples of motor level activity which add to his 'database' and which will eventually contribute to the development of his theories about the experiences he encounters and materials he explores. We can, however, deduce that George has an ability to get on 'with the business of learning', when he is free to build his own continuity and progression (Nutbrown 2011: 39) and the evidence of George's occupations present him as an 'active and independent' learner (40), and as a social actor in his life and learning.

Observation point:

When you watch young children in your setting, do you see children who are able to identify and select their own continuity and progression within their daily explorations? Is the environment rich in open-ended materials that children can use to explore and test out their ideas?

Do adults recognize children as active and independent learners?

Developing mastery: 'Going around'
(18th August; thirty-two months)

Initially George seemed a little unsure of my presence at his house today. I tried to give him time and space by spending time chatting with his parents and playing with his baby brother. In time, George signified his acceptance of my presence, by bringing his magnetic drawing toy to show me.

On this toy George could easily and quickly produce patterns and shapes.

George also had a paper pad of drawings that his mother shared; Figures 8.9 and 8.10 highlight the obvious similarity between his mark making endeavours. Georges mother explained that recently when she had asked George to put some kisses (X) in a birthday card, he had become very upset. The situation had been resolved through George drawing a smiley face inside the card.

When I last visited George at home he had demonstrated a distinct interest in using the farm fence to construct a boundary. This interest was still evident, and it was clear to me that his ability and building technique had greatly evolved. This time it took George only a couple of minutes to construct the fence panels as he had one on my previous visit demonstrated in Figure 8.7 with what seemed little effort.

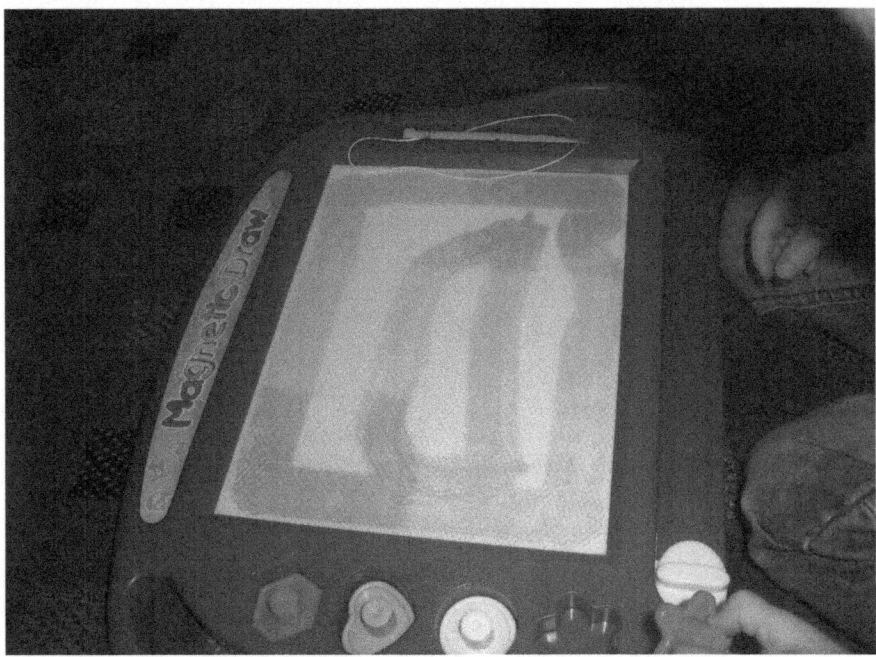

Figure 8.9 George's magnetic drawing

Figure 8.10 Drawings

This time once George had completed the construction of the fence panels, he set about placing all the animals inside the farm buildings. As George meticulously placed the animals within the farm buildings he said.

George: 'In you go…. just here… all in'

Once the animals had been placed to his satisfaction, he stood, seeming to admire his work. Then he walked around seeming to view from other angles; however he showed no interest in playing with the individual animals or farm set. He displayed no further interest in pursuing this activity. Instead George's attention turned to his Duplo.

George told me that he was going to 'build a house', and then proceeded to direct me to help search for the right sized bricks. As George connected the Duplo pieces together, he shared his thoughts and ideas on his construction 'A house… I build a house… you help me… need a window… the door is here'. George was orderly and methodical with the construction, taking his time. Selecting the correct brick sizes, he built systematically, completing one full row at a time. George's involvement continued for a further thirty-five minutes, the remainder of my afternoon visit. With regret I had to leave George before his house-building project was finished.

Discussion

Nutbrown (2011: 46) argues that it is only through 'looking closely' at children's actions that 'cognitive connections' can be recognized. George's 'cognitive connections' across the boundary of the nursery and his home have become visible. Whilst the content varies, thereby giving him extended nourishment for learning, his play environments provide opportunity for 'continuity' and 'progression' of thought within his schema.

George's obvious enjoyment and pleasure with his mark making endeavours is apparent through his eagerness to share his work and the numerous sheets completed in his drawing pad. Although at this point in time George does not share his thoughts in words, we can venture to suggest that there is perhaps a link between George's forms of thought, his interest in his surroundings, his going around a boundary and his 'mark making'. This implies that George is able to replay the movement patterns in his mind and represent them figuratively as marks.

George's forms of thinking over the last sixteen weeks have revealed themselves through his actions and exploration of water, tubes, sand, logs, bikes, prams, Duplo and farm sets. Athey (2007: 51) attributes such practice and repetition with high levels of cognitive confidence and knowledge that has been 'well assimilated'. It is from 'the fruits of his past encounters' (Atherton and Nutbrown 2013: 52) that George is able to create his future success as a skilled and playful mark maker.

Close analysis of George's mark making illustrates a developing mastery of his fine motor skill (Gardner 1984), providing evidence of both straight and curved lines. Yet when asked to draw an 'x' to represent a kiss, a symbol consisting of two intersecting slanted lines, George was un-compliant. A possible explanation for such agitation could be explained by Athey's (2007: 78) belief that 'most early marks are figurative outcomes of bodily movement'. This means that George understands that his marks and his graphical combinations of curved and straight lines have a figurative correspondence to his experiences, his movements and his forms of thought, his lived experiences. When asked to draw the symbol for a kiss (x), George was unfamiliar with this representation, this 'new knowledge' (51) that did not fit within his cognitive structures and his schemas, and this in unsurprising because the slanted line is the hardest for young children to represent and two intersecting slanting lines are even harder. George's behaviour during this task resonates with being placed within a level of 'cognitive discomfort' (51). Athey's (2007: 51) classification of such an experience describes the child as being placed within a functional level of a 'struggle', a long way from 'play' which comes with developed competence. The smiley face, however, fitted perfectly with George's mark making skills and his schematic focus. This illustrates how important it is that parents understand their own children's schemas and can adapt their interactions and expectations accordingly.

George now takes only a few moments to construct the three-dimensional boundary of the farm fence. Through 'the gradual evolution of schemas and the extension of early forms of thought' (Nutbrown 2011: 47), children form new ideas, and understanding. For George such understanding, together with his developing 'bodily intelligence', his developing 'mastery' of his finger movements (Gardner 1984: 207), has ensured his journey 'through the functioning ranges from struggle through to practice to play'. This means that now George can complete with what appears to be casual ease what was once considered to be a tricky task.

George's placing of the animals and his accompanying speech 'In you go' imply that this use of speech is not as a social tool (Piaget 1959: 17). George's aim seems not to be the engaging in a social conversation with other people, but rather his use of speech is to 'accompany, to reinforce' his actions. Conversely with the Duplo it could be suggested that George moves to a symbolic level, assimilating reality to self (Piaget and Inhelder 1969: 58), demonstrating his transition from representation of action to representation of thought. Accompanied by speech (symbols), George uses his knowledge of going round a boundary to recreate a house. George is able to think first about how to transform the plastic Lego bricks into a house with windows and doors, then he carries out his plan without need for trial and error at this stage (that came earlier). His ability to involve others and give instructions demonstrates his developing use of speech as a social tool (Piaget 1959). Atherton and Nutbrown (2013: 64) describe the actions of Henry, a child in the study as he uses a ball. Similar in age, there is parity in both Henry and George's use of language:

> Henry exchanged his thoughts with others and attempted to manipulate the behaviours of others in drawing the adult into assist him in his play, his schematic endeavours (64).

Athey (2007: 152) uses the term 'precise language', whilst Atherton and Nutbrown (2013: 64) refer to a 'dialogue of conceptual correspondence'. However, both agree that young children's language is further supported through accompanied language that matches forms of thought. George's parents at this time had been considering moving house. We do not know how much of these conversations George was part of, but such a match with his forms of thought would certainly have provided opportunity for George to assimilate appropriate language.

Observation point:

When watching children involved in play, consider their use of language. Do they speak as part of asocial interaction, using language as a social tool? Do they use language also to accompany, reinforce or affirm their actions?

Final thoughts

This chapter demonstrated how schemas authenticate George's individual thinking, as well as his cognitive development. Illustrating the high-level concepts, a thirty-month-old child 'came to know' when resources with people and things to follow his own intrinsic motivations. George's story demonstrates that through the use of open-ended opportunities to explore and create *he* was able to make important cognitive links, which help to clarify and consolidate his understanding of 'the nature of material objects in the world' (Gardner 1984: 18).

Many examples of George's own ability to recognize continuity are acknowledged, as he strived to form new ideas and gain a greater understanding through the coordination of his schemas. The chapter provides an opportunity to observe George's changing and developing cognitive structures, his 'development of conceptual' knowledge (Athey 2007: 29), as his previous experiences coordinate to form new more complex knowledge and understanding, new forms of thought. Through previous experiences with dynamic trajectory, as well as containing and enveloping, George's new interest of 'going through a boundary' and 'going around a boundary are revealed'.

Over the sixteen weeks, the observations provided a window into George's lived experiences, his play, as he went about his daily business of constructing and hypothesizing through fitting content to his schematic threads. George's story has a strong resonance with Atherton and Nutbrown's (2013: 139) consideration that 'the correlations, associations and relationships in children's thinking, revealed in their play, cannot be understood unless those observing have a conceptual awareness of what is seen'. Viewed independently, each individual observation provides only a fleeting glance into George's thinking. A conceptual awareness of George's forms of thought is not enough, the observer also needs a willingness to adjust and modify ideas 'in light of what [was] seen and heard' across the boundaries of space and time.

George's schema is proven to be a powerful tool in his journey of cognitive competence. His intrinsic self-motivation is exposed as both 'his pattern for action' (Neisser 1976: 56) and through his 'struggle' within his desire to master his fascinations with the log (Athey 2007: 192). The observations revealed George's developing mathematical notions of conservation and reversibility (Piaget and Inhelder 1969) – still only in his third year of life, at thirty-two months of age George's notions and understanding of high-level mathematical concepts. Such concepts will continue to remain imperceptible, in many young children if their learning is measured only against narrow and predetermined curriculum outcomes. George's story provides further evidence to support Nutbrown (2011) and Athey's (2007) arguments that the driving force in developing curricula for young children must be pedagogy.

In the next chapter we will look back on what we have learned from reflecting on the observations of Abby, Hannah, Emily and George and consider the implications for curriculum, pedagogy, partnership with parents and early childhood education policy.

Concluding Thoughts

In his local park there was a large mound, so large it might have been the Matterhorn to 28-month-old Jack. Jack liked the huge mound and enjoyed climbing it with the help of his eight-year-old sister Ashia. Several old, well-established trees grew on the mound, and Jack and Ashia walked round them, hugged them and hid between them. Playing in the trees on the mound was an important part of any visit to the park. To Jack looking up at the giants, it must have seemed as if these trees went on for ever into the sky. He liked to stand, very still, head back – looking up into the canopy of the trees high above him. Sometimes he wobbled a little – perhaps lulled into the swaying movement of the leaved in the breeze.

One day, when the family visited the park one of the great trees was lying on the ground with its fantastic roots (like branches themselves) exposed. It had fallen in a gale – the earth around it had been loosened with months of rain and it was finally felled during a high wind. Jack was fascinated by the felled tree, he seemed puzzled, went up to it, put his head on it and said a gently 'Ahhhh …' seemingly trying to comfort it as he wrapped his tiny arms around the huge girth of its trunk. Ashia said 'the tree's fallen down Jack. It fell in the storm'. Jack, still hugging the trunk repeated 'Tee down, tee down … fell down, tee down'. The fallen tree captured Jack's attention and he repeated 'tee down … fell down' several times, often pointing to the tree, during their time in the park that day.

At home later that evening Jack lay on the floor, very still. Ashia asked him – 'what are you doing lying so still Jack' … Jack said nothing, still lying, very still with his arms outstretched. Again Ashia asked 'Jack – what are you doing?' Eventually Jack said 'Tee … tee down … fell down …'.

Seeking to understand what young children do, and what their actions mean involves practitioners and parents in an endless quest to interpret their actions and identify what underpins the things that seem to grab children's attention. To recognize, understand and value young children's learning we need to know not only what they do but we need to crack their code. How do we look at what children are doing and make sense of it for ourselves? Understanding and interpreting children's actions to the point that we have strong clues about their learning is a bit like deciphering a coded message. The answer is there, but we need to know how to *read* what we see.

To *crack their code* we need useful and reliable theories, which we can use as reliable lenses through which we view what we see. When we recognize the learning underpinning certain actions we are in a position to reinforce and extend the opportunities for further learning. In Chapter 1 we briefly considered some theories of children's learning and in Chapter 2 we focused on Schema theory, showing how the persistent patterns in children's action, graphic and speech behaviours can be observed and understood as a clear and connected set of learning behaviours. We know that Jack was interested in the fallen tree, and it seems that he is representing the fallen tree himself by lying still on the ground, if his nursery practitioners knew this they might seek to extend this interest by talking more about trees in the park. They might, however, if they work with schemas in mind, offer Jack other opportunities to explore things that are upright and which fall such as building and demolishing brick towers. Schematic pedagogy offers a further dimension to extend young children's learning, and practitioners can ask themselves whether it is the *content* of trees that Jack is focusing on or whether it is the *form* of moving from vertical to horizontal that is the underpinning interest.

From the stories of Abby, Hannah, Emily and George we have seen how looking at learning with schemas in mind can provide adults with opportunities to acknowledge two-year-old children's capability to actively construct and develop an understanding of the world they live in. We have also seen how open-ended and flexible materials, with space and time to pose questions – in the same way that Isaacs (1930) encouraged the children at the Malting House School of the 1920s to do – can stimulate interesting and exciting learning episodes. Such an environment can create a learning ambiance that excites children to experiment and theorize; these are important elements in schematic pedagogy. We note that some of the most dynamic and extended learning episodes observed by Julie took place outside, using plentiful amounts of natural materials, with space to move, to pour, to walk, to run, to test out. In following the children from nursery setting to their home environments Julie was able to develop a greater understanding of how such young children were deeply motivated to explore their own ideas in those different spaces.

We want to make an important point here about the necessity of theory to effective practices in early childhood education. We are clear that our interpretation of the close observations of these children was only possible because of Athey's (2007) seminal work. Focusing mainly on three- to five-year-olds and their young siblings, her insights and schematic interpretations of how children moved, what they said, the marks they made and the stories and experiences they paid maximum attention to, underpin our own. Athey's (2007) Froebel Early Education Project was a groundbreaking contribution to our understanding of how young children, given good conditions and well-attuned and informed adults (both educators and parents), can construct their own learning, and pursue some quite complex ideas beginning with early motor and behaviours, through to the symbolic and thought level. For Athey (2007: 49) these forms of thinking were 'patterns of repeatable actions that lead to early categories and then to logical classifications'. Further, Athey (2013: 6) argues that

> Schemas transform the raw data of experience into meaningful and manageable units. Raw data is too messy and voluminous for the brain to deal with efficiently. Schemas sort out a large amount of data into fewer categories. Those categories, like later concepts, are easier to manage than trying to hold on to a heap of content.

Athey points out that when we take up interest in something new we find examples of it everywhere. For example, if a person takes up a new hobby, say gardening, then suddenly the television seems to have lots of gardening programmes and shops selling plants become very attractive. Or a family gets a new chocolate Labrador puppy, and suddenly there are chocolate Labradors feature in magazines, television programmes and in the parks! In the same way, for many women who are pregnant, shops selling baby clothes and equipment are ubiquitous, and baby advice and other babies seem to be everywhere! Athey points out that we notice content according to our interests, the content might have always been there but it is our interest in it that now makes it noticeable. She advises that: 'Schemas give content of a certain kind particular significance at particular times' (Athey 2013: 6).

So, when Abbey was exploring coverings, the things she used had long been part of her environment; and she used whatever was to hand to envelop or cover. Submerging her hands under water – but still being able to see them, covering her legs with jigsaw pieces or butterflies, pulling a net overhead and still being able to see through it (and to be seen). Abby was using these quite conventional materials in what might be considered unconventional ways.

What they were – was hardly (if at all) significant – *what Abbey could do with them*, was the thing that mattered. Abby was a powerful actor in her own learning and skilful manipulator of what she found at her disposal to rehearse ways of covering and being covered.

Hannah was fascinated with the numerous balls in the guttering. We think that she knew they should roll down and out at the bottom of the guttering, but the blockage caused them to stack up in a row in the guttering. And was there a connection between seeing numerous balls fitted into the guttering and her use of fitting opportunities during her heuristic play? Sometimes when things don't go to plan, or don't behave as children anticipate, this presents a new learning challenge which can promote new thinking. For some two-year-olds this can result in frustration, but it is interesting to see in Hannah's self-chosen persistence there is no hint of frustration. Whatever Hannah was thinking, we know that she was controlling and manipulating the objects she had selected from her environment and gaining visual feedback from her actions.

There seems to be a lot of *in and out* behaviour in Emily's story: when she contained the bubble-covered animals in the boot of the toy car, and her persistence in putting her feet *in and out* of her wellingtons – and the determination to learn the tricky skill of fastening buckles on her new shoes. Emily seems intent on finding out *what she can do* with the materials and opportunities that present themselves, as she strikes the balance between rewarding play and the struggle that sometimes ensures.

And George's fascination with the large piece of drift wood brought him back – time after time – to explore it. His repeated experimentation seemed at times to model the tenacity of a scientist repeating an experiment over and over again to test a new theory. Whatever was driving George, the materials and experiences available to him – as well as the time and space to continue his explorations – were crucial pedagogical elements that supported his learning.

The outdoor environment in the nursery provided an open ended, flexible and rich resource for the children to use to their own ends. We imagine that they formed numerous questions in their heads.... 'What can I do with this?', 'Where is the water gone?', 'Will I be able to see through this?'. We also consider that the flexibility and affordances of natural materials with space to try things out, move things around and 'test' ideas, is an important part of schematic pedagogy. What the children chose to explore were, in the main, on permanent offer in the nursery – the large piece of drift wood, the water butt and pipe, dolls, prams, cars, the slide and so on were always available. The children selected out, as Athey described, from what was available according to their prevailing interest and manipulated them to their own ends – often unconventionally. This exemplifies the assimilation of experiences as described by Piaget (1953: 384):

> Children do not just learn directly from aspects of environment. They learn by assimilation material, ideas and situations in the world into inner schemas and concepts.

Indeed it is not the setting or the environment alone that maximizes the possibility that children's true potential can be achieved. Parents themselves form a very important part of the process (Sylva et al. 2011); parents and professionals must develop a 'genuinely respectful' view of each other's knowledge (Athey 2007: 202) if children are truly to achieve their potential. The role parents and the home learning environment play in supporting young children's learning cannot be underestimated. Athey (2007: 201) describes how at the start of the Froebel Early Education Project (1973–1978) there existed a 'conceptual gulf' between practitioners and parents which was bridged by the development of 'genuine open-ended' inquiry to grow a shared understanding of children's patterns of cognition. An occurrence Julie also experienced during the work reported in this book. Hannah's exploits with the empty cups in Chapter 6 illustrate her mother's developing understanding of Hannah's patterns of cognition.

> *Hannah explored how to fit and stack the cups together. As Hannah explored, her mother supported and narrated the investigation.*
> *Mother: Hannah take care, these are real cups.*
> *Hannah: My cup, my cup in. My cup in Mum's.*
> *Mother: Yes it fits inside my cup …*

Hannah's mother's ability to recognize and gain a deeper understanding of her daughter's schematic interests (Nutbrown 2011: 29) provided her with a way to become more 'in tune' with her daughter, to adapt her actions and support her daughter's investigations and subsequent learning. A view reflected by Hannah's mother's own comments:

> I wouldn't have let her do that (stack the cups) before this (involvement in project). Now I understand better, I realise why she wants to put her truck on the TV cupboard. I find it really interesting, I have really started to watch her, I try to use my speech to support her ideas more.

Chapter 8 provides evidence of how George's mother also gained a greater insight and understanding of *how he* learns. George's refusal to draw kisses (x) in a birthday card initially confused and upset his mother. Only after discussing the episode with Julie did his mother appreciate that being asked to draw the symbol for a kiss (x) was something unfamiliar to George, yet allowing him to put a smiley face instead fitted with George's schematic focus at this time. Parental insight into such seemingly small cultural matters can be crucial in their understanding of their own children's participation in such practices.

Julie's experience demonstrates that when professionals share schematic pedagogy with parents, it provides parents with a deeper understanding and the possibility to adapt how they interact with their child. Following Athey's opening up of schematic theory to early years practitioners, others have continued to pay attention to young children's actions, speech and graphic representations and in doing so have been able to create forms of pedagogy which made a better match to young children's interests and behaviours (Arnold 2010; Atherton and Nutbrown 2013; Mairs and Arnold 2013; Meade and Cubey 2008; Nutbrown 2011). These have given us many meaningful accounts of children's schematic behaviour – what Athey and others have called 'schema spotting'. There have also been some attempts to demonstrate in highly practical ways how schemas can be incorporated into various early years curricula approaches such as the English *Early Years Foundation Stage* (Louis 2013) and New Zealand's *Te Whariki* (van Wijk 2008). This growing archive of observations, schematic interpretations and curriculum considerations adds to the richness of our knowledge about schematic underpinnings of children's learning and development and supports us as adults keen to facilitate deep, rich and meaningful learning to evolve appropriate pedagogical approaches. We can also see that different curricula approaches, if build on constructivist foundations, can usefully provide challenging *content* to children's schematic *forms*.

What Abbey, Hannah, Emily and George have shown us is that children who are still just two years of age, when viewed through a schematic lens can be powerful and persistent thinkers – if they have the environments that support them. They need their nursery, their home, their practitioners and their families to give them materials, time, space and support to explore, question, discover and create. They also need in those environments, adults who understand their learning patterns.

We know from very many studies that high-quality early childhood education can make all the difference to children's learning, development and well-being. More recently, studies focusing on babies and toddlers have highlighted the difference that attentive adults and positive learning spaces can make – the research spotlight that was once on three- to five-year-olds has, more recently, been shining brightly on the under threes. Atherton and Nutbrown (2013) have shown the power of using schema as a tool for interpreting the youngest children's thinking and understanding. As they explore the bits of the world that adults make available to them, the youngest children need attentive and knowledgeable adults to support them. Such adults should not intrude, or interfere, but rather observe and seek to interpret so as to understand what next supportive steps might be taken. What Atherton and Nutbrown (2016) set out as *schematic pedagogy* can be a useful way for practitioners to attune their practice to children under the age of three.

In this book we have glimpsed into the worlds of four two-year-olds, sharing in their learning journeys as they trod some new and unexplored territories and watching them finding in the world, things that fitted their own learning significances. As we have witnessed their learning worlds, we have learned from Abbey, Hannah, Emily and George how such young children's involvement with materials and the environment can support their schematic development and especially so when their adults, especially their parents are schema-attuned pedagogues.

Through the stories of Abbey, Hannah, Emily and George we can see how the continuities of their persistent schematic concerns thread through their thinking between home and the nursery. We have seen in their stories, clear links between opportunities for exploration and questioning in a rich and flexible environment, making the role of the adults in their learning clear and vital.

As Athey (2013: 11) notes:

> There is less difficulty in identifying schemas than there is in extending them. The most difficult of all is to start with very early schemas and to trace continuities to later aspects of the curriculum.

We suggest that there is a significant shift to be made for practitioners – and parents – to move from identifying – or 'spotting' – schemas to knowing how to nourish or extend them. We find the notion of schematic pedagogy (Atherton and Nutbrown 2016) helpful in this respect. Their indicators of schematic pedagogy include:

- *Unconventional beacons of possibility* which legitimize practitioners' descriptions of their practice with young children in creative and imaginative ways 'where mental and physical action is fuelled and where schemas may be pursued and nourished with relish' (13).
- *Paying careful attention to what matters to children* where practitioners use detailed observations to hone in on children's schemas so as to centre on 'the child and their individual thinking concerns' (13).
- *The tessellated nature of pedagogy* where adult and child 'fit' together and in so doing 'children's particular actions may take on new, perhaps unexpected significance if viewed through a schematic lens' and the 'individual characteristics of their play is understood both holistically and schematically' (13).
- *Knowledgeable, captivated accompaniment* where 'adults who partner children in play admire and appreciate the young proficients in their care, and endeavour to offer a worthy match' (14).

The notion of tessellation, where practitioners seek to *fit* their responsive practices to children's schematic concerns, implies a sense of *working out* – there is no template or single answer (as there would be in the act of fitting together pieces of a jigsaw) but it is more like building with bricks, where pieces are turned around and over, and tried into a space and moved to another until a meaningful whole is created. Meade (1995: 2) also put forward the notion of fitting pieces together. She too rejects the jigsaw metaphor preferring instead something more flexible:

> Perhaps the best metaphor is that schemas are like pieces of Lego which can be fitted in to lots of different structures, in this instance the structures are cognitive structures.

Perhaps those wonderful wooden three-dimensional bricks of different sizes and shapes provide the best metaphor. Not fixed, ever changeable and flexible according to children's interests.

This ability for practitioners to achieve a fit with the children they work with is crucial if they are to have a chance of understanding children's meanings. As Athey (2013: 9) notes:

> When children's schematic actions, rather than content, are observed, children's approaches to learning can be interpreted differently. It is through schemas and the fitting of content to different schematic threads that children's own constructions of reality and subsequent continuity can be identified.

We have seen Abby, Hannah, Emily and George fitting together numerous experiences as they combine to nourish their dominant schemas at the time. When early years practitioners are sufficiently confident in their understanding and interpretation of young children's schematic behaviours to achieve a good fit with those young minds, the learning that takes place will be rich and deep.

References

Abbott, L. and Langston, A. (2006). *Parents Matter: Supporting the Birth to Three Matters Framework*. Maidenhead: Open University Press.

Aldred, P. (1998). Ethnography and Discourse Analysis: Dilemmas in Representing the Voice of Children. In J. Ribbens and R. Edwards (eds), *Feminist Dilemmas in Qualitative Research: Public Knowledge and Private Lives*, pp. 147–170. London: Sage Publications.

Allen, G. (2011). *Early Intervention: The Next Steps. An Independent Report to Her Majesty's Government*. London: Cabinet Office.

Arnold, C. (2010). *Understanding Schemas and Emotion in Early Childhood*. London: Sage.

Athey, C. (1990). *Extending Thoughts in Young Children: A Parent Teacher Partnership*. London: Paul Chapman Publishing.

Athey, C. (2007). *Extending Thoughts in Young Children: A Parent Teacher Partnership* (2nd edn). London: Paul Chapman Publishing.

Athey, C. (2013). Beginning with the Theory about Schemas. In K. Mairs and C. Arnold (eds), *Young Children Learning through Schemas: Deepening the Dialogue about Learning in the Home and in the Nursery*. London: Routledge.

Atherton, F. and Nutbrown, C. (2013). *Understanding Schemas and Young Children from Birth to Three*. London: Sage.

Atherton, F. and Nutbrown, C. (2016). Schematic Pedagogy: Supporting One Child's Learning at Home and in a Group. *International Journal of Early Years Education*. DOI: 10.1080/09669760.2015.1119671.

Ball, C. (1994). *Start Right: The Importance of Early learning*. London: Royal Society of Arts.

Bartlett, F. C. (1958). *Thinking*. New York: Basic Books.

Baum, A., C. and Swick, K. J. (2008). Dispositions towards Families and Family Involvement: Supporting Pre-Service Teacher Development. *Early Childhood Education Journal*. 35. 579–584.

Biesta, G. (2009). Good Education in an Age of Measurement: On the Need to Reconnect with the Question of the Purpose of Education. *Education, Assessment, Evaluation and Accountability*. 21. 33–46.

Bowlby, J. (1997). *Attachment and Loss Volume 1*. London: Pimlico.

Bowlby, J. (1989). *The Making and Breaking of Affectionate Bonds*. Oxon: Routledge.

Brierley, J. (1994). *Give Me a Child until He Is Seven* (2nd edn). Lewes: Falmer Press.

Brooker, L. (2010). Learning How to Learn: Parental Ethnotheories and Young Children's Preparation for School. *International Journal of Early Years Education*. 11 (2). 117–128.

Bronfenbrenner, E. (1979). *The Ecology of Human Development: Experiments by Nature and Design*. Cambridge, MA: Harvard University Press.

Bruce, T. (2005). *Early Childhood Education* (3rd edn). London: Hodder Arnold.

Carr, M. (2001). *Assessment in Early Childhood Settings Learning Stories*. London: Sage.

Carr, M. and Lee, W. (2012). *Learning Stories Constructing Learning Identities in Early Education*. London: Sage.

Carr, M. and May, H. (2000). Te Whariki: Curriculum Voices. In H. Penn (ed.), *Early Childhood Services: Theory, Policy and Practice*, pp. 53–73. Buckingham: Open University Press.

Cassidy, J. and Shaver, P. (eds) (2008). *Handbook of Attachment Theory, Research and Clinical Application* (2nd edn). London: Guildford Press.

Chapman, A. J. and Foot, H. C. (eds) (1977). *It's a Funny Thing Humour*. Oxford: Pergamon Press.

Clandinin, D. J. (2006). Narrative Inquiry: A Methodology for Studying Lived Experience. *Research Studies in Music Education*. 27. 44–54.

Clare, A. (2012). *Creating a Learning Environment for Babies and Toddlers*. London: Sage.

Claxton, G. (2008). *Cultivating Positive Learning Dispositions*. University of Bristol: Unpublished Paper.

Claxton, G. and Carr, M. (2004). A Framework for Teaching Learning: The Dynamics of Disposition. *Early Years*. 24. 87–97.

Clough, P. and Nutbrown, C. (2007). *A Students Guide to Methodology, Justifying Enquiry* (2nd edn). London: Sage.

COAG. (2009). *Early Years Learning Framework for Australia (EYLF)*. Australian Government Department of Education, Employment and Workplace Relations for the Council of Australian Government. ISBN 978-0-642-77873-4.

Cole, M. (1998). Culture in Development. In M. Woodhead, D. Faulkner and K. Littleton (eds), *Cultural Worlds of Early Childhood*, pp. 11–33. London: University Press.

Corbetta, D. and Snapp-Childs, W. (2009). Seeing and Touching: The Role of Sensory-Motor Experience on the Development of Infant Reaching. *Infant Behavior and Development*. 32. 44–58.

David, T. (1996). Their Right to Play. In C. Nutbrown (ed.), *Respectful Educators – Capable Learners, Children's Rights and Early Education*, pp. 90–98. London: Paul Chapman.

David, T. Goouch, K. and Powell, S. (2016). *The Routledge International Handbook of Philosophies and Theories of Early Childhood Education and Care*. London: Routledge.

DCSF. (2009). *Learning, Playing and Interacting; Good Practice in the Early Years Foundation Stage*. Nottingham: DCFS Publications.

Degotardi, S. and Pearson, E. (2009). Relationship Theory in the Nursery: Attachment and Beyond. *Contemporary Issues in Early Childhood*. 10. 144–145.

DES. (1990). *Starting with Quality: Report of the Committee of Enquiry into the Quality of Education Experience Offered to Three- and Four-Year Olds* (Rumbold Report). London: HMSO.

Desfoges, C. and Abouchaar, A. (2003). *The Impact of Parental Involvement, Parental Support and family Education on Pupil Achievement and Adjustment: A Literature Review*. London: DfES.

DfE. (2011a). *Families in the Foundation Years Evidence Pack: Reference and Research Links for Families in the Foundation Years*. London: DfE.

DfE. (2011b). *Supporting Families in the Foundation Years*. Retrieved 17 November 2012 from: https://www.education.gov.uk/publications.

DfE. (2012). *More Great Childcare: Raising Quality and Giving Parents More Choice*. Retrieved 29 January 2013 from: https://www.education.gov.uk/publications/ standard/publicationDetail/Page1/DFE-00002-2013.

DfE. (2014). *Statutory Framework for the Early Years Foundation Stage: Setting the Standards for Learning, Development and Care for Children from Birth to Five*. Retrieved 5 February 2016 from: https://www.gov.uk/government/publications/ early-years-foundation-stage-framework--2.

DfEE. (1998). *Meeting the Childcare Challenge*. London: The Stationery Office.

DfES. (2002). *Birth to Three Matters – A Framework to Support Children in Their Earliest Years*. London: DfES.

DfES. (2003). *The National Standards for under 8s Day Care and Childminding*. Nottingham: DfES.

DfES. (2004). *Every Child Matters: Change for Children*. London: DfES.

DfES. (2007). *Early Years Foundation Stage: Setting the Standards for Learning, Development and Care for Children from Birth to Five*. Nottingham: DfES.

Dickson, L., Brown, M. and Gibson, O. (1993). *Children Learning Mathematics – A Teacher's Guide to Recent Research*. London: Cassell.

Dissanayake, E. (2015). *What Is Art For?* Washington: University of Washington Press.

Dockett, S., Einarsdottir, J. and Perry, B. (2009). Researching with Children: Ethical Tensions. *Journal of Early childhood Research*. 7 (3). 283–298.

Dockett, S. and Perry, B. (2007). Trusting Children's Accounts in Research. *Journal of Early Childhood Research*. 5 (1). 47–63.

Dowling, M. (2013). *Young Children's Thinking*. London: Sage.

Duffy, B. (2010). Introduction. In G. Pugh and B. Duffy (eds) *Contemporary Issues in The Early Years*, pp. 1–5 (5th edn). London: Sage.

Dweck, C. (1999). *Self Theories: Their Role in the Motivation, Personality, and Development*. Philadelphia: Psychology Press.

Early Education. (2012). *Development Matters in the Early Years Foundation Stage (EYFS)*. London: DfE.

Edwards, S. (2006). Stop Thinking of Culture as Geography: Early Childhood Educators' Conceptions of Sociocultural Theory as an Informant to Curriculum. *Contemporary Issues in Early Childhood*. 7 (3). 238–252.

Edwards, C., Gandini, L. and Forman, G. (1998). *The Hundred Languages of Children: The Reggio Emilia Approach Advanced Reflection* (2nd edn). Westport: Ablex.

Edwards, C., Gandini, L. and Forman, G. (2011). *The Hundred Languages of Children: The Reggio Emilia Experience in Transformation* (3rd edn). Oxford: Praeger.

Edwards, C. P., Knoche, L., Aukrust, V., Kumru, A. and Kim, M. (2005). *Parental Ethnotheories of Child Development: Looking beyond Independence and Individualism in American Belief System*. Faculty Publications, Department of Child, Youth, and Family Studies. University of Nebraska Paper 10. Retrieved 22 March 2012 from: http://digitalcommons.unl.edu/famconfacpub/10.

Elfer, P., Goldschmied, E. and Selleck, D. (2012). *Key Persons in the Early Years: Building Relationships for Quality Provision in Early Years Settings and Primary Schools*. London: Routledge.

Elkind, D. (1969). Piagetian and Psychometric Conceptions of Intelligence. *Harvard Education Review*. 39 (2). 319–37.

Erikson, E. (1950) *Childhood and Society*. New York: Norton.

Evangelou, M., Sylvia, K., Kyriacou, M., Wild, M. and Glenny, G. (2009). *Early Years Learning and Development*. Research Report RR176: DCSF.

Fargas-Malet, M. McSherry, D., Larkin, E. and Robinson, C. (2010). Research with Children: Methodological Issues and Innovative Techniques. *Journal of Early Childhood Research*. 8 (2). 175–192.

Feinstein, L. (2003). Inequalities in Early Cognitive Development of British Children in the 1970 Cohort. *Economica*. 70. 73–97.

Field, F. (2010). *The Foundation Years: Preventing Poor Children Becoming Poor Adults*. London: Cabinet Office.

Forman, G. (1994). Different Media, Different Languages. In L. G. Katz and B. Cesarone (eds), *Reflections on the Reggio Emilia Approach*, pp. 185–211. Chicago: ERIC Clearinghouse on Elementary Early Childhood Education.

Furth, H. G. (1969). *Piaget and Knowledge: Theoretical Foundations*. London: Prentice-Hall.

Gandini, L. (1998). History, Ideas, and Basic Philosophy. In C. Edwards, L. Gandini and G. Forman (eds), *The Hundred Languages of Children: The Reggio Emilia Approach, Advanced Reflections* (2nd edn). Westport: Ablex Publishing 49–97.

Gardner, H. (1984). *Frames of Mind the Theory of Multiple Intelligences*. London: Heinemann.

Gerhardt, S. (2004). *Why Love Matters: How Affection Shapes a Baby's Brain*. London: Routledge.

Goldschmied, E. and Jackson, S. (2004). *People under Three, Young Children in Day Care* (2nd edn). Oxon: Routledge.

Gopnik, A., Meltzoff, A. and Kuhl, P. (1999). *How Babies Think*. London: Weidenfeld and Nicolson.

Graham, P. (2009). *Susan Isaacs: A Life Freeing the Minds of Children*. London: Karnac Books.

Greenland, P. (2000). *Hopping Home Backwards: Body Intelligence and Movement Play*. Leeds: Jabadao Publication.

Hall, K., Horgan, M., Ridgway, A., Murphy, R., Cunneen, M. and Cunningham, D. (2010). *Loris Malaguzzi and the Reggio Emilia Experience*. Continuum Library of Educational Thought. Volume 23. London: Continuum.

Harkness, S. and Super, C. M., (1992). Parental Ethnotheories in Action. In I. V. Sigel, A. V. McGillicuddy-Delisa and J. Goodnow (eds), *Parental Belief Systems: The Psychological Consequences for Children*, pp. 373–392 (2nd edn). Oxon: Routledge.

Hayes, N. (2008). Teaching Matters in Early Educational Practice: The Case of Nurturing Pedagogy. *Early Education and Development*. 19 (3). 430–440.

Hedges, H. and Cullen, J. (2012). Participatory Learning Theories: A Framework for Early Childhood Pedagogy. *Early Child Development and Care*. 182 (7). 921–940.

Howard, J., Bellin, W. and Rees, V. (2002). *Eliciting Children's Perceptions of Play and Exploiting Playfulness to Maximise Learning in the Early Years Classroom*. Proceedings of the 2002 BERA Annual Conference, pp. 1–14.

Hughes, A. (2006). *Developing Play for the under 3s: The Treasure Basket and Heuristic Play*. London: David Fulton.

Inhelder, B. and Piaget, J. (1964). *The Early Growth of Logic in the Child: Classification and Seriation*. London: Routledge and Paul Kegan.

Isaacs, N. (1930). 'Why Questions' Appendix pp. 291–349. In S. Isaacs (ed.), *The Intellectual Growth of Young Children*. London: Routledge and Kegan Paul.

Isaacs, S. (1930). *Intellectual Growth in Young Children*. London: Routledge.

Janzen, M. D. (2008). Where Is the (Postmodern) Child in Early Childhood Education Research? *Early Years an International Journal of Research and Development*. 28 (3). 287–297.

Johnson, M. (1987). *The Body in the Mind: The Bodily Basis of Meaning, Imagination and Reasoning*. Chicago: Chicago University Press.

Katz, L. (1988). What Should Young Children Be Doing? *American Educator*. (Summer). 29–45.

Kellett, M. (2010). *Rethinking Children and Research: Attitudes in Contemporary Society*. London: Continuum.

Lahman, M. K. E. (2008). Always Othered Ethical Research with Children. *Journal of Early Childhood Research*. 6 (3). 281–300.

Lam, M. S. and Pollard, A. (2007). A Conceptual Framework for Understanding Children as Agents in the Transition from Home to Kindergarten. *Early Years: An International Journal of Research and Development*. 26 (2). 123–141.

Laevers, F. (1976). *The Project Experiential Education: Concepts and Experiences at the Level of Context, Process and Outcome*. Retrieved 23 June 2013 from: https//www .european-agency.org/agency-projects/assessment…/at…/file.

Laevers, F. (1994). *Defining and Assessing Quality in Early Childhood Education*. Belgium: Laevers University Press.

Laevers, F. (2000). Forward to Basics! Deep-Level Learning and the Experiential Approach. *Early Years*. 20 (2). 20–29.

Laevers, F. (2011). Experiential Education: Making Care and Education More Effective through Well-Being and Involvement. *Encyclopedia on Early Childhood Development*. Retrieved February. 2016 from: www.child-encyclopedia.com/Pages/ PDF/LaeversANGxp1.pdf.

Louis, S. (2013). *Schemas and the Characteristics of Effective Learning*. London: British Association for Early Childhood Education.

Mairs, K. and Arnold C. (eds) (2013). *Young Children Learning through Schemas: Deepening the Dialogue about Learning in the Home and in the Nursery*. London: Routledge.

MacNaughton, G. (2005). *Doing Foucault in Early Childhood Studies: Applying Poststructural Ideas*. Oxon: Routledge.

Malaguzzi, L. (1998). History, Ideas and Basic Philosophy: An Interview with Lella Gandini. In C. P. Edwards, L. Gandini and G. Forman (eds), *The Hundred Languages of Children: The Reggio Emilia Approach Advanced Reflection*, pp. 48–98 (2nd edn) Westport: Ablex.

Matthews, J. (2010). *Drawing and Painting Children and Visual Representation* (2nd edn). London: Sage.

May, H. (2001). *Politics in the Playground*. Wellington: Bridget Williams Books.

McMillan, M. (1919). *The Nursery School*. London: Biblio Life, Reprint (2009).

McVee, M., Dunsmore, K. and Gavelek, J. (2005). Schema Theory Revisited. *Review of Educational Research*. Winter 2005, 75 (4). 531–566.

Meade, A. (1995). *Thinking Children*. Wellington: New Zealand Council for Educational Research.

Meade, A. and Cubey, P. (2008). *Thinking Children Learning about Schema*. New York: Open University Press.

Meade, A. and Podmore, V. N. (2003). *Early Childhood Education Policy Co-ordination under the Auspices of the Department/Ministry of Education: A Case Study of New Zealand*. Paris: UNESCO Early Childhood and Family Education Unit.

Melhuish, E. C., Phan, M. B., Sylva, K., Siraj-Blatchford, I. and Taggart, B. (2008). Effects of Home Learning Environment and Preschool Center Experience upon Literacy and Numeracy Development in Early Primary School. *Journal of Social Issues*. 64 (1). 95–114.

Ministry of Education. (1996). *Te Whariki. Early Childhood Curriculum*. Wellington: Learning Media.

Moss, P. (2010). We Cannot Continue as We Are: The Educator in an Education for Survival. *Contemporary Issues in Early Childhood*. 11 (1). 8–19.

Moyles, J. (2010). *The Excellence of Play* (3rd edn). Maidenhead: Open University Press.

Munn, P. (1987). Children's Beliefs about Counting. In I. Thompson (ed.), *Teaching and Learning Early Numbers*, pp. 9–19. Buckingham: Open University Press.

Neisser, U. (1976). *Cognition and Reality Principles and Implications of Cognitive Psychology*. San Francisco: Freeman and Company.

Nutbrown, C. (1996). *Respectful Educators – Capable Learners: Children's Rights and Early Childhood Education*. London: Paul Chapman.

Nutbrown, C. (2010). Naked by the Pool? Blurring the Image? Ethical Issues in the Portrayal of Young Children in Arts-Based Educational Research. *Qualitative Inquiry*. 17 (3). 3–14.

Nutbrown, C. (2011). *Threads of Thinking Schemas and Young Children's Learning* (4th edn). London: Sage.

Nutbrown, C. (2013). *Shaking the Foundations of Quality? Why 'Childcare' Policy Must Not Lead to Poor Quality Early Education and Care*. Retrieved 9 July 2013 from: http://www.shef.ac.uk/polopoly_fs/1.263201!/file/Shakingthefoundationsofquality.pdf.

Nutbrown, C. and Clough, P. (2013). *Early Childhood Education: History, Philosophy and Experience*. London: Sage.

Page, J. (2016). The Legacy of John Bowlby's Attachment Theory. In T. David, K. Goouch and S. Powell (eds), *The Routledge Handbook of Philosophies and Theories of Early Childhood Education and Care*. London: Routledge.

Page, J., Clare, A. and Nutbrown, C. (2013). *Working with Babies and Children from Birth to Three* (2nd edn). London: Sage.

Page, J. and Nutbrown, C. (2008). *Working with Babies and Children from Birth to Three*. London: Sage Publications.

Park, J. H. and Kwon, Y. I. (2009). Parental Goals and Parenting Practices of Upper-Middle-Class Korean Mothers with Preschool Children. *Journal of Early Childhood Research*. 7 (1). 58–75.

Payne, G. and Isaacs, L. (2008). *Human Motor Development: A Lifespan Approach* (7th edn). New York: McGraw-Hill.

Penderi, E. and Petrogiannis, K. (2011). Parental Ethnotheories and Customs of Childrearing in Two Roma Urban Communities in Greece: Examining the Developmental Niche of the 6-Year Old Child. *Journal of Social, Evolutionary, and Cultural Psychology*. 5 (1). 32–50.

Percy-Smith, B. and Thomas, N. (2010). *A Handbook of Children and Young People's Participation Perspectives from Theory and Practice*. Oxon: Routledge

Piaget, J. (1950). *The Language and Thought of the Child*. London: Routledge and Kegan Paul.

Piaget, J. (1952). Jean Piaget (Autobiography). In E. G. Boring (ed.), *A History of Psychology in Autobiography*, Vol. 4, pp. 237–256. Worcester MA: Clark University Press.

Piaget, J. (1953). *The Origins of Intelligence in the Child*. London: Routledge and Kegan Paul.

Piaget, J. (1959). *The Language and Thought of the Child*. London: Routledge and Kegan Paul.

Piaget, J. (1970). *Structuralism*. New York: Basic Books.

Piaget, J. (1972). *The Psychology of the Child*. New York: Basic Books.

Piaget, J. (1990). *The Child's Conception of the World*. New York: Littlefield Adams.

Piaget, J. and Inhelder, B. (1969). *The Psychology of the Child*. London: Routledge and Kegan Paul.

Pink, S. (2007). *Doing Visual Ethnography* (2nd edn). London: Sage.

Pugh, G. (2010). Improving Outcomes for Young Children: We Can Narrow the Gap. *Early Years; International Journal of Research and Development*. 30 (1). 5–14.

QCA. (2000). *Curriculum Guidance for the Foundation Stage*. London : QCA.

Rayna, S., and Laevers, F. (2011). Understanding Children from 0 to 3 Years of Age and Its Implications for Education. What's New on the Babies' Side? Origins and Evolutions. *European Early Childhood Education Research Journal*. 19 (2). 161–172.

Ring, K. (2010). Supporting a Playful Approach to Drawing. In P. Broadhead, J. Howard and E. Wood (eds), *Play and Learning in the Early Years*, pp. 113–125. London: Sage.

Ritchie, J. and Buzzelli, C. (2012). Te Whāriki – The Early Childhood Curriculum of Aotearoa New Zealand. In N. File, J. J. Mueller and D. B. Wisneski (eds), *Curriculum in Early Childhood Education. Re-examined, Rediscovered, Renewed*, pp. 146–159. New York and London: Routledge.

Robert, R. (2010). *Wellbeing from Birth*. London: Sage Publications.

Robert-Holmes, G. (2012). It's the Bread and Butter of Our Practice: Experiencing the Early Years Foundation Stage. *International Journal of Early Years Education*. 20 (1). 30–42.

Robson, S. (2012). *Developing Thinking and Understanding in Young Children. An Introduction for Students* (2nd edn). Oxon: Routledge.

Rogers, C. and Freiberg, H. J. (1993). *Freedom to Learn* (3rd edn), New York: Merrill.

Rogoff, B. (1990). *Apprenticeship in Thinking Cognitive Development in Social Context*. Oxford: University Press.

Rogoff, B. (1998). Cognition as a Collaborative Process. In W. Damon (ed.), *Handbook of Child Psychology, Volume 2, Cognition, Perception, and Language*, pp. 679–744 (5th edn). New York: Wiley.

Rosen, R. (2010). 'We Got Our Heads Together and Came Up with a Plan. *Journal of Early Childhood Research*. 8 (1). 89–108.

Ross, T. (2016). *David Cameron Plans Parenting Classes for All Parents*. Telegraph. Retrieved 11 January 2016 from: http://www.telegraph.co.uk/news/newstopics/eureferendum/12091327/David-Cameron-plans-parenting-classes-for-all-families.html.

SCAA. (1996). *Desirable Outcomes for Children's Learning on Entering Compulsory Education*. London: DfEE and SCAA.

Scott, W. (1996). Choices in Learning. In C. Nutbrown (ed.), *Respectful Educators – Capable Learners Children's Rights and Early Education*. London: Sage.

Shore, B. (2002). Taking Culture Seriously. *Human Development*. 45. 226–228.

Siraj-Blatchford, I. and Manni, L. (2008). Would You Like to Tidy Up Now? An Analysis of Adult Questioning in the English Foundation Stage. *Early Years*. 28 (1). 5–22.

Skinner, B. F. (1974). *About Behaviorism*. Knopf : Vintage.

Smidt, T. (2006). *The Developing Child in the 21st Century: A Global Perspective on Child Development*. Oxon: Routledge.

Soler, J. and Miller, L. (2010). The Struggle for Early Childhood Curricula: A Comparison of the English Foundation Stage, Te Whariki and Reggio Emilia. *International Journal of Early Years Education*. 11 (1). 57–68.

Springate, I., Atkinson, M., Straw, S., Lamont, E. and Grayson, H. (2008). *Narrowing the Gap in Outcomes: Early Years (0–5 years)*. Slough: NFER.

Super, C. M. and Harkness, S. (1986). The Developmental Niche: A Conceptualization at the Interface of Child and Culture. *International Journal of Behavioral Development*. 9. 545–569.

Super, C. M. and Harkness, S. (2002). Cultural Structures: The Environment for Development. *Human Development*. 45. 270–274.

Sylva, K., Melhuish, E., Sammons, P., Siraj-Blatchford, I. and Taggart, B. (2008). *Effective Pre-school and Primary Education 3-11 Project (EPPE 3-11). Report from the Primary Phase: Pre-school, School and Family Influences on Children's Development during Key Stage 2 (Age 7–11)*. DCSF Research Report 061. Retrieved 6 March 2011 from: http://www.ioe.ac.uk/newsEvents/16439.html.

Sylva, K., Melhuish, E., Sammons, P., Siraj-Blatchford I. and Taggart, B. (2011). Pre-school Quality and Educational Outcomes at Age 11: Low Quality Has Little Benefit. *Journal of Early Childhood Research*. 9 (2). 109–124.

Sylva, K., Melhuish, E., Sammons, P., Siraj-Blatchford, I., Taggart, B. and Elliot, K. (2004). *The Effective Provision of Pre-school Education Project: Findings from the Pre-school Period*. London: University of London.

Taggart, B. (2010). Making a Difference: How Research Can Inform Policy. In K. Sylva, E. Melhuish, P. Sammons, I. Siraj-Blatchford and B. Taggart (eds), *Early Childhood Matters: Evidence from the Effective Pre-school and Primary Education Project*, pp. 206–223. London: Routledge.

Tickell, C. (2011). *The Early Years: Foundation for Life, Health and Learning*. London: DfE.

Trevarthen, C. (2012). Finding a Place with Meaning in a Busy Human World: How Does the Story Begin, and Who Helps. *European Early Child Education Research Association Journal*. 20 (3). 303–312.

United Nations. (1989). *Conventions on the Rights of the Child*. Retrieved 5 November, 2012 from: www.unhchr.ch/html/menu3/b/k2crc.htm.

Van Wijk, N. (2008). *Getting Started with Schemas: Revealing the Wonderful World of Children's Play*. Waitakere, New Zealand: New Zealand Play Centre Federation.

Vygotsky, L. S. (1978). *Mind in Society*. Cambridge, MA: Harvard University Press.

Vygotsky, L. S. (1980). *Mind in Society: The Development of Higher Psychological Processes*. Cambridge: Harvard University Press.

Vygotsky, L. S. (1986). *Thought and Language*. Cambridge: MIT Press.

Wallerstedt, C. and Pramling, N. (2011). Learning to Play in a Goal-Directed Practice. *Early years: An International Journal of Research Development*. 32 (1). 5–15.

Warin, J. (2011). Ethical Mindfulness and Reflexivity: Managing a Research Relationship with Children and Young People in a 14-Year Qualitative Longitudinal Research (QLR) Study. *Qualitative Inquiry*. 17. 805–814.

Whalley, M. (2010). Forward. In C. Arnold (ed.), *Understanding Schemas and Emotion in Early Childhood*, pp. xii–xiv. London: Sage.

Winnicott, D. (1953). Transitional Objects and Transitional Phenomena. *International Journal of Psychoanalysis*. 34. 89–97.

Wood, E. (2013). *Play, Learning and the Early Childhood Curriculum*. London: Sage.

Wood, E. and Attfield, J. (2005). *Play, Learning and the Early Childhood Curriculum*. London: Sage.

Wood, E. and Hall, E. (2011). Drawing as Spaces for Intellectual Play. *International Journal of Early Years Education*. 19 (3–4). 267–281.

Author index

Subject index